MACMILLAN MODERN DRAMATISTS

TOM STOPPARD

Thomas R. Whitaker

Professor of English
Yale University

First published 1983 by
THE MACMILLAN PRESS LTD
London and Basingstoke
Companies and representatives throughout the world

ISBN 0 333 28502 6 (hc)
ISBN 0 333 28503 4 (pbk)

Typeset by WESSEX TYPESETTERS LTD, Frome, Somerset

Printed in Hong Kong.

Contents

List of Plates

Editors' Preface

The *Macmillan Modern Dramatists* is an international series of introductions to major and significant nineteenth- and twentieth-century dramatists, movements and new forms of drama in Europe, Great Britain, America and new nations such as Nigeria and Trinidad. Besides new studies of great and influential dramatists of the past, the series includes volumes on contemporary authors, recent trends in the theatre and on many dramatists, such as writers of farce, who have created theatre 'classics' while being neglected by literary criticism. The volumes in the series devoted to individual dramatists include a biography, a survey of the plays, and detailed analysis of the most significant plays, along with discussion, where relevant, of the political, social, historical and theatrical context. The authors of the volumes, who are involved with theatre as playwrights, directors, actors, teachers and critics, are concerned with the plays as theatre and discuss such matters as performance, character interpretation and staging, along with themes and contexts.

BRUCE KING
ADELE KING

for
Tom, Sarah Mae, Mary Beth, and Gwen

1

Centres of Levity

When *Rosencrantz and Guildenstern Are Dead* was first performed on the fringe of the Edinburgh Festival in August 1966, Ronald Bryden announced 'the most brilliant debut by a young playwright since John Arden'. The next April, when it was produced in London by the National Theatre, Harold Hobson called it 'the most important event in the British professional theatre of the last nine years'. Arden's social concern, John Osborne's anger, and even Harold Pinter's comedy of menace were beginning to seem moods of the past. For the moment, at least, the 'university wit' of this non-university journalist, who had rewritten *Hamlet* as if from a back-stage Beckett's-eye-view, was all the rage. And indeed, during the next several years Tom Stoppard managed to come up with one surprising whirlwind of verbal and theatrical levity after another.

In 1968 he had two plays on the London stage, the earlier *Enter a Free Man* and a new one-act farce, *The Real Inspector Hound*. In 1970 came another one-act farce,

After Magritte, and in 1972 his second major play, *Jumpers*. Reaching for high comedy now, Stoppard engaged ideas no less metaphysical than those puzzling Rosencrantz and Guildenstern but more obviously pertinent to an agnostic and technocratic society. In 1974 came his third major play, *Travesties*, an astonishing concoction of theatrical pastiche and serious inquiry into art and politics. Along the way there had also been other pieces in several media. Stoppard was clearly establishing himself as a major presence in the theatre – some hybrid of W. S. Gilbert and Oscar Wilde, perhaps, who had received an education in Bernard Shaw, James Joyce, Evelyn Waugh, T. S. Eliot, Noel Coward, Samuel Beckett, and N. F. Simpson. There were critics, of course, who still thought him a self-indulgent Scrabble-player unwilling or unable to engage the problems of the world on its own solemn terms. But surely no recent British or American playwright could compete with Stoppard's wit, his talent for pastiche and parody, and his ability to shape intellectual debate into a dazzling three-ring circus.

Who was this young master of levity? He was born on 3 July 1937, in Zlín, Czechoslovakia, as Tomas Straussler, the second son of a company doctor for Bata shoe manufacturers. In 1939, just before the Nazi invasion of Czechoslovakia, Dr Eugene Straussler was prudently transferred to Singapore, taking his family with him. In 1942, when the Japanese invaded Singapore, Martha Straussler and her sons were evacuated to India. (Dr Straussler, remaining behind, was killed.) In Darjeeling young Tomas attended a multilingual boarding school, while his mother managed a Bata shoe shop. Late in 1945 she married a British Army major, Kenneth Stoppard, who soon took the family with him back to England. Tom Stoppard, as he now became, attended Dolphin School in

Nottinghamshire and Pocklington School in Yorkshire. In 1954 he obtained a job as a junior general reporter for the *Western Daily Press* of Bristol, where his family had now settled. Four years later the *Bristol Evening World* hired him as a reporter, feature writer, and drama critic. In 1960 he began to support himself by freelancing as he wrote plays. His first play, *A Walk on the Water*, was produced on British Independent Television in 1963. By then Stoppard was writing short stories, working as drama critic for the short-lived London magazine *Scene*, and doing some other pieces for it under the name of 'William Boot'. (Boot is that provincial journalist in Evelyn Waugh's *Scoop* who is mistakenly sent to Africa. His name would haunt Stoppard's early farces, and *Scoop* itself would later help to shape *Night and Day*.) In 1964 Stoppard wrote short plays and serial episodes for Radio 4, went to Berlin on a Ford Foundation Grant, and began a one-act verse play called *Rosencrantz and Guildenstern Meet King Lear*. The next year he wrote weekly episodes for *A Student's Diary,* a BBC Radio serial about an Arab in London, saw his second play, *The Gamblers*, produced at Bristol University, completed *Rosencrantz and Guildenstern Are Dead*, and wrote a novel, *Lord Malquist and Mr Moon*. During the same year he also married Jose Ingle; but the marriage would later end in divorce, with Stoppard retaining custody of his two sons. (In 1972 he would marry Dr Miriam Moore-Robinson, and would soon thereafter have two more sons.) In 1966, after having been taken on option by several companies, *Rosencrantz and Guildenstern Are Dead* was finally performed in Edinburgh by the amateur Oxford Theatre Group. At the age of twenty-nine, Stoppard was launched on his new career.

Stoppard shares with Joseph Conrad and Vladimir

Nabokov a brilliantly detached mastery of English. No doubt his journalistic apprenticeship inclines him toward a lively accessibility that might cause those masters to raise an eyebrow, but he is above all a stylist, with the irony and anxiety that come with that vocation. Indeed, it has taken him some time to outgrow his playful role as a Wildean aesthete. 'Some writers write because they burn with a cause which they further by writing about it,' he said in a piece of 1968 called 'Something to Declare'. 'I burn with no causes. I cannot say that I write with any social objective. One writes because one loves writing.' In 1972 he said to Mel Gussow: 'I write plays because dialogue is the most respectable way of contradicting yourself'. Even in 1974, after the writing of *Jumpers* and *Travesties*, he could report to Ronald Hayman his 'comical reaction' to the charge that his plays are not political: 'I think that in the future I must stop compromising my plays with this whiff of social application. They must be entirely untouched by any suspicion of usefulness. I should have the courage of my lack of convictions.'

That arch declaration echoes not only Wilde but also the amiable but anxious bachelor don in Christopher Hampton's *The Philanthropist*. At one point, in what Stoppard once called his favourite line in modern English drama, Philip says: 'My trouble is, I'm a man of no convictions. . . . At least, I think I am'. Later, after discovering his own excessive respect for other people's opinions, he admits: 'I haven't even got the courage of my lack of convictions'. Stoppard has fastened on Philip as a wry rendering of his own more vigorously self-doubting dubiety. He knows, of course, that every self-professed man of no convictions does in fact have certain unrecognised or unadmitted assumptions that guide his acts, and he understands his own inveterate self-contradiction as a dialectical strength. 'I don't respect people who are rigorously consistent', he told Gussow in 1972. 'That denotes a kind of atrophy of spirit.' As Stoppard has made his own assumptions more and more explicit, he has moved pretty steadily to increase that 'whiff of social application'. Indeed, in another interview of 1974, 'Ambushes for the Audience', he could say: 'Briefly, art . . . is important because it provides the moral matrix, the moral sensibility, from which we make our judgements of the world'. By 1977 he was making a good many political statements, and could declare himself in a book-review a supporter of 'Western liberal democracy, favouring an intellectual élite and a progressive middle class and based on a moral order derived from Christian absolutes'. Two years later he said to Gussow: 'I'm conservative with a small c. I'm a conservative in politics, literature, education, and theatre.' And he now described his dialectical spirit less flippantly: 'I don't write plays with heroes who express my point of view. I write argument plays. I tend to write for two people rather than for One Voice.'

Stoppard's more recent plays have often reflected this emerging recognition of his own convictions. In 1977 a piece for actors and orchestra, *Every Good Boy Deserves Favour*, engaged the Soviet repression of liberty of speech, and a television play, *Professional Foul*, dealt with the same problem as it had appeared in Czechoslovakia. In 1978 *Night and Day* set forth a debate on the freedom of the press. And in 1979 *Dogg's Hamlet, Cahoot's Macbeth* treated with childlike verve the attempt in Czechoslovakia to prevent free expression. But those plays were not simply topical, and their variety of tone and mode makes it evident that Stoppard remains an exploratory stylist, ready to bring his talent and craft to bear upon a remarkably wide range of assignments. Indeed, his most recent adaptations, from Schnitzler and Nestroy, have no direct connection at all with political topics. It seems likely, therefore, that we will not understand at any depth the intellectual and stylistic diversity of Stoppard's continuing career unless we can formulate its essential unity of aim.

I shall suggest in this book that, from *Rosencrantz and Guildenstern Are Dead* through *Dogg's Hamlet, Cahoot's Macbeth* and *On the Razzle*, Stoppard has been variously engaged in a single task. He has been exploring the playfulness to which he early committed himself, and has been gradually articulating the convictions that inform such a commitment. If we rethink his development in these terms, we will find that his recent work elucidates what his highly verbal but also significantly non-verbal theatre games have long been doing.

'Plays are events rather than texts,' he said to Gussow in 1979. 'They're written to happen, not to be read.' Stoppard's 'events' ask the director, actors, and witnesses to collaborate in imagining and interpreting actions that may seem to result from a wildly free invention but actually obey a hidden rationale. Often one or more of the characters, drawn into some fantastic plot that elucidates a hitherto unrecognised condition, can serve to suggest our own role in such games. If we accept the invitation to modify our merely spectatorial distance, and to join the actors in playing all roles with a sympathetic but detached imagination, we soon find ourselves up to our necks in a usually hilarious trouble. And that trouble illuminates some of the self-deceptions or confusions into which our culture has tempted us. Such an exposure of our condition does not imply a doctrine imposed upon the dramatic material. It results from the dialectical rationale of each event, which is a version of the larger rationale that governs all playful exploration. The norms of Stoppard's theatre games are in fact the norms of play itself.

Stoppard's 'levity' therefore buoys us up with more than that word usually suggests: this 'lightness' approaches 'light'. In *Artist Descending a Staircase*, a radio play of 1972 that is among other things a conversation about modern art, a blind woman named Sophie utters this bit of wisdom: 'But surely it is a fact about art – regardless of the artist's subject or his intentions – that it celebrates a world which includes itself – I mean, part of what there is to celebrate is the capability of the artist'. To that remark the artist Martello, lost in what a friend will later call 'the child's garden of easy victories known as the avant-garde', can only respond: 'How very confusing'. Stoppard's plays will gradually unconfuse us on this important matter, as they celebrate through their difficult structures not just one man's capability but our shared power of entering into such collaborative worlds of play.

At mid-career, Tom Stoppard has amply demonstrated what can be done by a self-styled entertainer who has assimilated the recent tradition of British comedy and learned much from the formal discoveries of the avant-garde. Like W. S. Gilbert, he can parody with ease the absurdities of his time. Like Noel Coward, he keeps his eye on the popular stage as he attends to 'those weary, Twentieth Century Blues'. Like Bernard Shaw, he knows that the stage at its best does not set before us photographs of 'real people' but invites us to participate in stylised explorations of our intellectual and emotional life. And like Oscar Wilde, who was himself far more than an aesthete, Stoppard knows what it means to write 'a trivial play for serious people'. His wit is often touched by an intellectual chill, a mordant fantasy, or an inarticulate pang that suggests the presence of Samuel Beckett. But his plays also complicate their artifice with various strategies that invite our intimate approach. Eliciting from actors and witnesses a more various participation than either Wilde or Beckett would have endorsed, they begin to turn the theatre itself into the model of a playful community. They ask us to accept as a finality neither Wilde's delightfully brittle world of masks nor Beckett's exhilaratingly austere world of fragmentation and deprivation. Alert to the possibility of dwelling in those worlds among others, they invite us to rediscover the humane balance and freedom that constitute the open secret of play.

2

Anxious Stylists

Who are Stoppard's stylists? Some of them – Lord Malquist, the Player in *Rosencrantz and Guildenstern Are Dead*, Sir Archibald Jumper in *Jumpers*, Tristan Tzara in *Travesties* – dazzle us with their panache. They are role-players who seem to have become the dandified roles on which they lavish their attention. Narcissists and often professed nihilists, they show few signs of anxiety, having dissolved that inconvenient emotion in the acids of style. Though hungering for an audience, they project images of sophisticated self-sufficiency. Certain others – George Riley in *Enter a Free Man,* Mr Moon, Rosencrantz and Guildenstern, Birdboot and Moon in *The Real Inspector Hound*, George Moore in *Jumpers*, Henry Carr in *Travesties* – are more appealing in their oddness and bumbling earnestness. No less concerned to elaborate a mask or invent a world, they have not known how to divorce themselves from the homely texture of our moral experience. Their ineptitude betrays the connections between a longing for style and an anxiety arising from loneliness, ineffectuality, or loss of meaning. Yet others – Jane Moon in *Lord Malquist and Mr Moon*, Dorothy Moore in *Jumpers*, the musician Ivanov in *Every Good Boy Deserves Favour* – seem even less consciously in control of their own projects. Anxiety itself has overwhelmed their faculties, turning what might once have been persons into riddling images of what has not been faced. In their incoherence and exhibitionism we may hear strange cries for help. Even the most ordinary people in a Stoppard work tend to be at least unconscious stylists. Linda in *Enter a Free Man*, Gladys in *If You're Glad I'll Be Frank*, Brown in *A Separate Peace*, Albert in *Albert's Bridge*, and Ruth Carson in *Night and Day* all employ their modest talents in constructing or seeking out an order of existence that has for them a secret distinction.

The strategies of these stylists, of course, are various. They may take refuge in an artifice of words or manners, try to invent themselves out of language, set in motion a rhetorical dialectic, play verbal games as they wait for an apocalyptic resolution of their uncertainties, or simply gravitate uncomprehendingly toward some rigid and reductive order. But all tacitly assume that style is our main clue to meaning – or can at least enable us to cope with a chaotic, oppressive, or loveless world. Their author, too, may seem to act on the same assumption. In rendering his stylists' behaviour, however, he alters its import. Setting style against style, he lets them illuminate each other. And by inviting us into his more inclusive game, he transforms each character's self-isolating play into a means of shared insight.

Stoppard's early portrayals of such stylists already focus his most important themes. His first play, *A Walk on the Water,* was written soon after he had quit his regular job

with the Bristol *Evening World* in 1960. It was adapted for
television in 1963, presented on stage in Hamburg in 1964,
and then revised as *Enter a Free Man* for its London
premiere at the St Martin's Theatre, where it was directed
by Frith Banbury. Its rather anticlimactic appearance in
1968, after the success of *Rosencrantz and Guildenstern
Are Dead*, was the unplanned result of its being produced
at the tail-end of a two-year option. Stoppard has called it
his 'Flowering Death of a Cherry Salesman' and has said
that its characters are 'only real because I've seen them in
other people's plays'. But, though *Enter a Free Man* does
frequently echo both Arthur Miller's *Death of a Salesman*
and Robert Bolt's *Flowering Cherry*, it is very much a
Stoppard play.

Its protagonist, George Riley (played by Michael
Hordern in the original production), is a fifty-year-old
inventor of nothing useful, who remains afloat thanks to
his daughter's job at Woolworth's, his wife's tidy home-
making, and his own wilful buoyancy. Like Miller's Willy
Loman, he is nourished by clichés and by visions of
commercial success. Like Jim Cherry, he talks of a bold
step into freedom that he will never take. Like both, he has
a sympathetic wife, and a rebellious child who punctures
his airy pretensions. Riley's wife, however, has long ago
made him chuck the security of a regular job – a step that
Cherry's wife urges in vain at the end of Bolt's play – and
Riley now talks of leaving his wife and daughter. In fact,
he simply will not admit that for years he has been trying to
create the world mainly out of his own imagination. He
has invented a bottle-opener that will open no bottles, a
pipe that will never go out if smoked upside down, a clock
that plays 'Rule, Britannia', an envelope gummed on both
sides of its flap, and a device to provide indoor plants with
the equivalent of outdoor rain. But though he does not

11

realise it, his most successful inventions have been acts of self-persuasion. The theme of the sustaining 'life-lie', of course, had entered Ibsen's *The Wild Duck,* Gorki's *The Lower Depths*, and O'Neill's *The Iceman Cometh* before Miller and Bolt adapted it to a mid-century domestic realism made flexible by transparent walls and multiple playing areas. For Stoppard it became in part a way to explore through comic displacement his anxiety about the fate of someone who quits his job and launches a free-lance career on the basis of sheer verbal inventiveness.

The exploration makes use of a counterpoint among several worlds. Dominating the stage is the world of Riley himself, a lonely but gregarious dreamer, outrageously ebullient, stubborn in his refusal to listen, and sometimes petulant or trembling with self-doubt, but almost never at a loss for words. Indeed, his rhetoric leads him by the nose. When speaking to a woman just met in a pub, he bogs down in redundancy: 'After all, the whole point of being an inventor is that you are inventing something that has never been invented before, otherwise what's the point of inventing it?' But he can leap at once into a sea of romantic clichés:

Florence, look at me. You see a man standing on the brink of great things. Below me, a vast flat plain stretches like an ocean, waiting to receive my footprints, footprints that will never be erased, and in years to come, people will see this once uncharted untrod path and say . . . George Riley walked this way. . . .

And in a confident moment at home with his wife, he can achieve the slickness of media hype:

How can I help being excited! For centuries while the

12

balance of nature has kept flower gardens thriving with alternate sun and rain in the proportions that flowers understand, indoor plants have withered and died on a million cream-painted window-sills, attended by haphazard housewives bearing arbitrary jugs of water. For centuries. Until one day, a man, noticing the tobacco-coloured leaves of a dessicated cyclamen, said to himself, what the world needs is indoor rain.

So erratic a style can approach many insights but make none its own. Riley lectures his daughter Linda with a volley of admonitions that might apply to himself: 'Headlong. Out of your death. You think each moment's going to last forever and then you're brought down with a bump. You never learn. . . . Watch where you're going. Take stock. Test the ground. Don't jump in with your eyes shut. That's the way you get hurt.' In the pub he sketches a vision that almost admits his ignorance of any world beyond that of his own imagination:

If we were each born into a separate room and had to stay in it, by the time we died we'd know every corner of it. But the world we take on trust. How do I know that Japan really exists? Or Tahiti. Or America or Morocco – or *Manchester*?

And, after stalking and berating a mild customer named Brown whom he imagines an industrial spy about to steal his double-gummed envelope, he can roundly declare: 'Now look here – I don't care if your name is Smith or Jones or Robinson. . . . The question is – *what are you playing at*?'

The question is a boomerang. With such stylistic resources, Riley hardly needs others to convict him of fabricating his own world. That matter of 'naming' is central to his own predicament. By the play's end, he begins to recognise that he has been more alert to his whimsical acts of naming than to the real names of others. It is part of Stoppard's game to conceal from us at first the fact that Riley has named for himself, and so for us, his wife Persephone (whose real name is Constance), the young sailor Able (who is really Dick), and the barman Carmen (who is Victor). Then, at the height of Riley's confidence in his imagined partnership with Harry, a gambler who has feigned an interest in his envelope, he realises that he lacks a crucial detail: 'We'll be a big business one day . . . our name will mean something . . . *Riley and* . . . [*Pause*] . . . Hey, what's Harry's other name?' In a few minutes Harry will dash Riley's hopes, and Able will laughingly recall that important symptom: 'You didn't even know his name . . .'.

In ironic contrast to the world Riley spins about himself as a defence against self-knowledge, Stoppard has set those of Persephone and Linda, who seem at first more limited but more perceptive. That contrast soon moves, however, toward a more deeply ironic disclosure of similarities. Persephone has shut herself into a meagre world of unexamined actions. Her life has become an anxious routine of tidying up, the 'point' of which she cannot explain. Paradoxically, the sameness of her life has acquired much of its difficulty because she once urged Riley to act upon his presumed 'difference' and so risk failure. And yet, though admiring that 'difference', she cannot really define it. Her dogged fidelity is a compulsive style that operates within the narrow limits of the undefined. Linda, who is lively, unsentimental, and self-ironic, rebels against her mother's dreary 'sameness' as well as her father's irresponsible 'difference'. But she understands that Riley's self-conscious role-playing is a strategy of survival: 'The point is, what's he like? I mean when we can't see him. He's got to be different – I mean you wouldn't even *know* me if you could see me – . . . . And that goes for everyone. There's two of everyone.' She also seems detached enough from her own emotions to talk lightly of her latest romantic affair, with a thirty-year-old motorcyclist. But by the end of the play she has anxiously risked elopement and has been deceived more seriously than her father. Riley was right: she too has been projecting a dream. The ironic similarity comes home to us when her self-recognition echoes Able's final taunt to Riley: 'All that talking and loving – I thought I *knew* him – I thought I knew everything about him. . . . I didn't even know his name'. The style of slapdash adolescence has been as vulnerable to self-deception as that of histrionic middle age. If there is any hope for freedom within the mainly self-closed worlds of *Enter a Free Man*, it lies in the final hesitant rapport between the emotionally bruised and perhaps somewhat wiser father and daughter.

As a theatrical event, however, *Enter a Free Man* offers a more hopeful understanding of how freedom may enter such worlds. Balancing sympathy and distance, its semi-realistic form prevents us from remaining firmly inside or outside of any individual world. At stage-right we see the Riley living-room, at stage-left the old-fashioned pub. Act One gives us from several view-points the meaning of Riley's oscillations between the two. The brief opening scene between Persephone and Linda, just after he has left the house one Saturday noon, soon dovetails into the longer second scene, which begins with his arrival at the pub. The momentary counterpoint between the two scenes already suggests, in Chekhovian manner, the 'talking past each other' that will paradoxically unite all the characters.

After Riley has encountered Harry, his imagined partner-to-be, Brown, his imagined adversary, and Florence, his imagined soul-mate, the second scene modulates into his memory. A long speech to Florence about home soon becomes a soliloquy half-addressed to us from centre-stage and then leads into a conversation between Riley and Persephone that has occurred prior to the opening moments of the play. Once established, this scene proceeds as if in the present: Linda comes downstairs, she and Riley have a lengthy spat, Riley leaves, and Act One comes full circle with a verbatim repetition of the opening scene and its dovetailing into the second. The oscillating and circular dramatic form has encouraged our fluid participation in the entire action and helped us to maintain a balanced sympathy with all three members of the Riley family.

Stylistic modulations in the pub scene also expand our sense of play among these self-closed worlds. As Riley bounces from one customer to another, inviting Able's naïve admiration and Harry's amused contempt, he suggests that those in his on-stage and off-stage audiences are dreamers like himself. He dictates a sardonic note to Able's 'Carissima Silvana', attacks Harry's gambling as the 'opiate of the common herd', and mounts a tirade against modern times: 'Dreams! The illusion of something for nothing. No wonder the country is going to the dogs'. When Harry ironically plays along with that diatribe and Carmen chimes in with antiphonal responses, however, the very nature of the dialogue seems to change, and we begin to follow a game of satirical ping-pong that soon acquires absurdist overtones:

HARRY: Look at the Japanese!
RILEY: The Japanese look after the small inventor!
HARRY: All Japanese inventors are small.

CARMEN: They're a small people.
HARRY: Very small. Short.
RILEY: The little man!
HARRY: The little people!
RILEY: Look at the transistor!
HARRY: Very small.
RILEY: Japanese!
CARMEN: Ghurkas are short.
HARRY: But exceedingly brave for their size.
CARMEN: Fearless.
RILEY [*furiously*] What are you talking about!

The illusion of realism, already worn thin by the dovetailing of scenes, becomes the mask for a playfulness beyond that of any character. A related effect occurs minutes later, when Riley begins to stalk the presumed spy, Brown. In an aside to Able, Riley has compared his own achievement with that of Edison in inventing the lighthouse:

BROWN [*unexpectedly*]: Edison didn't invent the lighthouse, you know. You probably got mixed up with Eddystone.
RILEY: What?
BROWN [*bashfully half-singing, smiling hopefully, explaining*]: My-father-was-the-keeper-of-the-Eddystone-light-and-he-met-a-mermaid-one-fine-night . . .
[*A terrible silence*]
RILEY: Your father was what?
BROWN: Not my father.
RILEY: Whose father?
ABLE: You can bet it wasn't a real mermaid.

17

RILEY: Shut up. [*To* BROWN] Whose father was a mermaid?

BROWN: He wasn't a mermaid. He *met* a mermaid.

The misunderstanding builds until Riley declares: 'What your father saw was a sea lion'.

BROWN: My father didn't see a sea lion!

RILEY [*topping him*]: So it was your father!

The brisk ineptitudes and empty victories of the music-hall have taken on something of Stoppard's obsessive verbalism. After such preparation, Riley's own rhetoric can approach virtuoso heights without our complaining that realism is being violated. The world of each character's style is a field for Stoppard's playful freedom – and ours.

The events of Act Two, on the following day, repeat the oscillation from home to pub and back, but without the dovetailing scenes and circular structure. The linear movement emphasises the finality of Riley's and Linda's departures and the climatic shattering of their hopes – and also suggests that the future need not repeat the past. Riley may act on his hesitant decision to register at the Labour Exchange, though he cadges another five shillings from Linda, and he and Linda may now understand each other. But those are slender possibilities. We have seen nothing here of any world beyond home and pub. The main suggestions of off-stage reality – Linda's planned motorcycle ride to Gretna, Able's remembered dance with Silvana in Naples, Harry's and Florence's proposed jaunt to Epsom – are as self-deceiving as Riley's dreams. Rather as in Chekhov's plays, isolated but analogous dreamers are yearning for an illusory off-stage richness of life. Beckett had already abstracted that pattern from the surrounding world and filled it with a more insistent comic energy at odds with the bleak vision of closure. In Stoppard's play, behind the resemblances to Miller and Bolt, we can detect a similar impulse as the playful energy in which we participate transforms the lonely worlds portrayed.

Even the London reviewers disappointed by the 'thinness' of this 'mainstream' play, in comparison with *Rosencrantz and Guildenstern Are Dead*, could not resist the histrionic volatility of Michael Hordern's Riley. 'Hordern imposed himself completely from the moment he made his first entrance into the pub,' said Mary Holland. 'His manner is confidential as he cons a drink, his eyes brighten with sudden light, glaze to hopelessness, his jowls quiver with excitement of new possibilities.' But Hordern was not simply using *Enter a Free Man* as a vehicle for his own considerable talents. He was taking part in its playful design. That fact was recognised by reviewers more alert to Stoppard's intentions. After granting the differences between this play and *Rosencrantz and Guildenstern Are Dead*, J. W. Lambert insisted that here too Stoppard:

> performs amazing feats of virtuosity, blending everyday inanities with flights of even more ridiculous fancy, linking his delightful chop-logic with the tarnished cliches of the saloon bar. . . . And in Michael Hordern he found the actor to send his conversational flourishes, his imaginative flights, whizzing round the theatre like steel balls round a pin-table. Here, from author and actor alike, came an exhilarating exhibition of how to spin a certain gaiety from despair and absurdity. . . .

The freedom of *Enter a Free Man* inheres less in the worlds it represents than in the collaborative play it invites us to share.

Stoppard's next play, *The Gamblers*, explored yet more boldly if less successfully the power of free-wheeling rhetoric. (It was presented by the Drama Department of Bristol University in 1965 but remains unpublished. Excerpts are quoted in Ronald Hayman's *Tom Stoppard*.) Stoppard there traded one kind of obvious indebtedness for another, as he partly recognised when dubbing *The Gamblers* his 'Waiting for Godot in the Condemned Cell'. Two nameless characters, a condemned prisoner and a jailer-executioner, have been thrown together by the fortunes of political revolution. Their anxious joking recalls Beckett's *Waiting for Godot*, but their longer speeches and driving passions recall Jean Genet's *Deathwatch* and *The Balcony*. Because they want to play extreme roles and each has a passion for his own opposite, the action follows a Genet formula: the executioner, deciding that the martyr's glory is of supreme importance, finally puts on the hood of the condemned man, who puts on the executioner's mask. Stoppard once described the play as 'all mouth'. But its extreme rhetorical stances, political and metaphysical themes, and complementary and reversible characters point forward to *Rosencrantz and Guildenstern Are Dead*, *Travesties*, and *Every Good Boy Deserves Favour*.

Three short stories that Stoppard wrote during 1963 and published in 1964 also contain anxious stylists who hope to create their lives out of rhetoric. The lonely man in 'Reunion', who tries to persuade an old girl-friend to rejoin him, confesses his belief in a strange verbal magic that might introduce some meaning into his alienated life:

'There is a certain word,' he said very carefully, 'which if shouted at the right pitch and in a silence worthy of it, would nudge the universe into gear. You understand me, it would have to be shouted in some public place dedicated to silence, like the reading room at the British Museum, it must violate it, a monstrous, unspeakable intrusion after which nothing can be the same for the man who does it.'

The protagonist of 'Life, Times: Fragments' is more sophisticated. A journalist and writer of fiction, he arrogantly dismisses all previous writers and seeks an absolute originality. His first-person paragraphs, however, are literary pastiche – with Hemingway and Beckett being most prominent. And even the narrator's third-person prose, which may be written by the protagonist himself as he imagines his foundering career, affects a self-consciously derivative style. In sharp contrast, the narrator of 'The Story' has accepted the style and ethos of commercial news, the human costs of which he obliquely documents. In flat cadences that ineffectively deny his moral complicity, he tells how he was persuaded to help publicise the conviction of a schoolmaster for molesting a little girl, and how the resulting notoriety led to the schoolmaster's suicide. With an irony reminiscent of Ring Lardner, Stoppard here portrays the insensitive world against which all of his more original characters will rebel with absurd incompetence or odd-ball brilliance.

During the next three years, as Stoppard's talent for witty eclecticism began to find its own direction, his work gained rapidly in sophistication and complexity. In 1964, after completing two fifteen-minute radio plays for the BBC, *The Dissolution of Dominic Boot* and *'M' Is for Moon among Other Things*, he spent some months in West Berlin as one of four young playwrights sponsored by the Ford Foundation. While there he wrote a one-act verse burlesque, *Rosencrantz and Guildenstern Meet King Lear*,

Tom Stoppard

which by early in 1965 he had drastically revised and expanded into a full-length play. In *Rosencrantz and Guildenstern Are Dead* the doomed playfulness of anxious stylists who 'aren't there', in several senses, has become the field for the more freely collaborative presence of actors and audience. And as that play was being performed in Edinburgh in the summer of 1966, an elaborate novel, written shortly after the play's completion, appeared in print. In *Lord Malquist and Mr Moon*, Stoppard had orchestrated a brilliant array of absurd stylists. For him as for James Joyce or Vladimir Nabokov, fiction had now become a parodic and self-parodic game between writer and reader. As it happens, *Lord Malquist and Mr Moon* sold less than five hundred copies in 1966 and sales were helped out in the bookshops only by the smashing success of *Rosencrantz and Guildenstern* in London the following year. But the playful course of Stoppard's career was now set.

During those years of rapid development, Stoppard also wrote simpler pieces for radio and television that explore the linked themes of style and anxiety. The thirty-minute radio play, *If You're Glad I'll Be Frank*, written for a BBC series on strange occupations and broadcast in February 1966, translates the predicament of the unconscious stylist into terms that exploit the auditory medium. Gladys works as the voice of TIM, the 'speaking clock' that announces to British telephone-customers the passage of every ten seconds. As the human equivalent of an endless tape, she is split between two styles: the mechanical announcement of the time and a free-verse inner monologue that reflects upon her dizzy awareness of time's flow. Her external situation recalls the early plays of Eugene Ionesco, with their images of middle-class conformity as an absurd tyranny, but her inner monologue approaches a pastiche of

22

T. S. Eliot's 'The Love Song of J. Alfred Prufrock' or *Four Quartets*. Gladys's schizoid style is linked to her psychological ambivalence: she both resists and welcomes the emptily chronometric order to which she is confined. Though agnostic, she had once tried to withdraw from chaos to a nunnery, and she now speaks from the ambiguous secular retreat provided by the Post Office. As she does so, her husband Frank, a London bus-driver, recognises her voice and tries to reach her through the baffles set up by the postal bureaucracy. This ingenious plot, complicated by Frank's need to maintain his own rigid schedule on the bus-route and by his inadvertent exposure of the sexual indiscretions being committed by stuffy bureaucrats, dramatises hilariously and poignantly the hypnotic power of a social order that asks us to repress all awareness of its lack of meaning. Gladys responds to that power with introverted bewilderment and panic; Frank attacks it with bluff vigour and an increasingly farcical frenzy. But both are trapped in the repetitive structure that is also, for us, the playful vehicle of insight.

A television play of August 1966 develops an aspect of that situation more simply. *A Separate Peace* sounds like an Ernest Hemingway title, and indeed the enigmatic stylist in this play is looking for what Hemingway called 'a clean, well-lighted place'. Confident but secretive, John Brown installs himself in a nursing home. 'It's the privacy I'm after,' he says, '– that and the clean linen.' His case is a puzzle. 'But there's nothing wrong with you!' exclaims the Matron. 'That's why I'm *here*,' says Brown. In fact, he has experienced his own version of Hemingway's *nada*:

MATRON: What have you been doing?
BROWN: Nothing.

MATRON: And what do you want to do?
BROWN: Nothing.

One understands how Stoppard could be the proud possessor of a first edition of Hemingway's *In Our Time*. Like Gladys, John Brown has unsuccessfully sought refuge in a religious institution. 'What I need is a sort of monastery for agnostics'. He also has fond memories of a quiet stretch as prisoner of war. And if he were an eccentric millionaire, this minimal stylist would give his retreat from chaos a magnificent elaboration in a hospital all for himself. As he develops that fancy, the laconic Brown seems strangely like the more verbally expansive Lord Malquist.

Albert's Bridge, a sixty-minute radio play first produced in July 1967, locates itself between such analogous extremes. In Albert, Stoppard has summed up the main traits of all his anxious stylists: he is evasive but creative, inclined toward an aesthetic transcendence of life's insoluble problems, and half-consciously flirting with self-destruction. Unable to stay on at the university after receiving his degree, Albert has taken a temporary job as a painter on the Clufton Bay Bridge. He says to his mother:

It's absurd, really, looking down on the university lying under you like a couple of bricks, full of dots studying philosophy. . . . What could they possibly know? I saw more up there in three weeks than those dots did in three years. I saw the context. It reduced philosophy and everything else. I got a perspective. Because that bridge was – separate – complete – removed, defined by principles of engineering which makes it stop at a certain point, which compels a certain shape, certain joints – the whole thing utterly fixed by the rules that make it stay up. It's complete, and a man can give his life to maintenance, a very fine bargain.

Work that others may find tedious, profitless, or even insane has for him the qualities of a major artistic endeavour.

Albert's great chance comes when the Bridge Sub-Committee, confused by the slightly specious mathematics of the City Engineer, tries to save money by replacing a team of four painters who apply a two-year coat of paint with a single painter who will apply an eight-year coat. Taking the job, Albert settles at once into a life-time career. He celebrates its attractions by crooning to himself in free verse:

> Dip brush, slide, stroke,
> it goes on as smooth and shiny
> as my sweat. I itch.
> Paint on my arm,
> silver paint on my brown arm;
> it could be part of the bridge.

His narcissism is strangely self-creating and world-creating:

> Listen. The note of Clufton is B flat.
> The whole world could be the same.
> Look down, is it a fact
> that all the dots have names?

In that flat and anonymous world below, Albert has dropped out of his middle-class family and neglects his wife Kate, the maid whom he had married after almost inadvertently getting her pregnant. When he takes Kate on a brief trip to Paris, he can only fall in love with the audaciously useless thrust of the Eiffel Tower. Back on his bridge, he meets one day a fellow-spirit, an extreme image of his own condition. Paranoid, apocalyptic, and suicidal, Fraser has climbed the bridge to escape the swarming and swelling chaos below. He had intended to jump, but he now finds the world quite small and safe. Reassured by his new vision of 'dots and bricks, giving out a gentle hum', Fraser descends – but only to return in the days that follow, again and again, like a yo-yo.

Neither a lifetime commitment nor a frenetic vacillation can save such anxious stylists from the chaos they fear. The apocalypse foretold by Fraser arrives one day when both men are on the bridge. The Sub-Committee has realised its mistake – the old two-year coat of paint is deteriorating more rapidly than one man can replace it – and has decided to send up an army of eighteen-hundred painters to finish the job at once. Whistling 'Colonel Bogey', they march in step out onto the bridge, setting up a vibration that pops its rivets, releases its taut girders, and sends the whole structure crashing into the bay. The world's roar, reduced for a while to the pleasant hum in the ears of these stylists, has reasserted itself with a vengeance. *Albert's Bridge* offers a condensed translation into auditory terms of the dilemma that Stoppard had already elaborated in *Lord Malquist and Mr Moon,* where the committed narcissist and the vacillating paranoid, brothers in spirit, meet a more complex fate.

Stoppard's only novel has remained his most complicated though not his most powerful work. In the summer of 1966, as he later told Janet Watts, he believed that *Rosencrantz and Guildenstern Are Dead* would be of little consequence whether it succeeded or failed at Edinburgh but that *Lord Malquist and Mr Moon* would make his reputation. And if we compare this novel with others of the mid-sixties that aim at parodic and self-parodic dark comedy, it seems quite accomplished. It is more finely wrought if less ambitious than John Fowles's *The Magus*, has a sharper wit and a more polished style than Thomas Pynchon's second novel, *The Crying of Lot 49,* and is intellectually as impressive as John Hawkes's fourth novel, *Second Skin.* Nevertheless, when *Lord Malquist and Mr Moon* evokes erotic passion, moral disorder, or apparent meaninglessness, it manages to be witty without being haunting or compelling. To a large extent, however, that effect of hollowness is designed.

In 1895 Oscar Wilde had been driven to his jury-trial in a two-horse carriage equipped with a brilliantly outfitted coachman and a powdered page. On what we must infer to be 29 and 30 January 1965, Lord Malquist rides somewhat hazardously about London in a pink and yellow coach that is drawn by a pair of greys in silver-studded harness and equipped with a black coachman in mustard livery. Like Wilde, Lord Malquist is an oral stylist who holds that calculated excess is true economy, an acute social commentator who lives deliberately and outrageously beyond his financial and moral means, and a romantic aesthete who plays at being a Restoration dandy. Like his fictive predecessors, Don Quixote and Stephen Dedalus, he is also accompanied by an earthier partner. Unwilling to set down his own aphorisms, he has hired Mr Moon to be his Boswell. Writing to Moon on the day of the death of an unnamed national hero, whom we must infer to be Winston Churchill, he has offered a moral rationale for their collaboration. Because the age of men of action is past, the heroic posture must now be 'that of the Stylist, the spectator as hero, the man of inaction who would not dare roll up his sleeves for fear of creasing the cuffs'. In these precarious times, an inbred and disengaged aesthetic is a virtue:

> We all have an enormous capacity for inflicting harm, and hereto the only moral issue has been the choice of the most deserving recipient. But the battle is discredited and it is time to withdraw from it. I stand aloof, contributing nothing except my example.

Much of the time, however, his example seems that of moral insensitivity or self-anaesthesia.

Nor does his project result in anything publishable. Moon is a Boswell who cannot recognise allusions to Dr Johnson and who, at the typewriter, has 'no natural style'. In fact, he is a self-declared historian unable to get past the first sentence of his ambitious history of the world, a husband unable to consummate his marriage, and a man of agonised moral sensitivity who goes about London with a live bomb in his coat-pocket. Like young Arthur in Slawomir Mrozek's *Tango*, which Stoppard adapted (in Nicholas Bethell's translation) for production by the Royal Shakespeare Company in 1966, Moon combines a wistful longing for traditional order and an imperfectly repressed tendency toward paranoid violence. Like the Lord High Executioner in Gilbert and Sullivan's *The Mikado*, he has a little list. And like the bomb-carrying and mentally defective Stevie Verloc in Joseph Conrad's *The Secret Agent*, he will finally be blown up. Moon does not seek vengeance, however, but what he calls 'purgation' or 'salvation'. As he tells Long John Slaughter, one of two fake cowboys who ride about London promoting Western Trail Pork 'n' Beans:

It is not simply a matter of retribution, it is a matter of shocking people into a moment of recognition – *bang!* – so that they might make a total re-assessment, recognise that life has gone badly wrong somewhere, the proportions have been distorted, I hope I make myself clear?

Moon's consciousness is filled with Joycean verbal games, Eliot-like ruminations on the meaning of life, sexual visions divorced from articulate emotion, and an increasingly intense – and ironically quite justified – fear that the swarming confusion of London will overwhelm him. He is himself a kind of 'spectator as hero', a lesser Leopold Bloom on the edge of sanity. Only when smashed on the head with an eighteenth-century gilt mirror or otherwise rendered unconscious can he know what it is 'to solve the world'.

Although the combination of talents represented by Lord Malquist and Mr Moon is not auspicious, a great deal takes place on the two days that climax with the state funeral of the unnamed national hero. Moon tries without success to take down Lord Malquist's oral compositions; the coach accidentally runs down and kills a certain Mrs Cuttle, the wife of an anarchist; Lord Malquist lays amorous if impotent siege to Moon's exhibitionistic but apparently frigid wife Jane; one of the fake cowboys, who fancy themselves rivals for Jane's affections, accidentally shoots her French maid, Marie; Moon assaults and kills an elderly General who is taking an indiscreet photograph of Marie's corpse; an Irishman who proclaims himself the Risen Christ is persuaded by Moon to carry off both corpses, wrapped in a carpet, on the back of his donkey; Moon himself, somewhat cut up by broken glass, is relieved of his virginity by Lord Malquist's childless and dipsomaniac wife Laura; the members of Lord Malquist's household, alerted to his imminent bankruptcy, depart forthwith; the cowboys finish each other off in a farcical but messy shoot-out; Moon's bomb, much to his surprise, turns out to be a grandiosely obscene toy; and Moon finally catches a real bomb that has been tossed by Mr Cuttle into Lord Malquist's coach. 'The horses bolted again, dispersing Moon and O'Hara and bits of pink and yellow wreckage at various points along the road between the Palace and Parliament Square.'

Neither Lord Malquist nor Mr Moon is a spokesman for Stoppard, though both express with absurd distortion some of the book's serious concerns. Lord Malquist pretends to withdraw with style from the chaos, and he can be brightly callous about those deaths for which he is responsible: 'I am always bumping into people'. But he can also be a fairly shrewd moralist, even about style. Beau Brummel, he tells Jane, 'understood that substance is ephemeral but style is eternal . . . which may not be a solution to the realities of life but it is a workable alternative'. Workable? He adds after a moment's brooding: 'As an attitude it is no more fallacious than our need to identify all our ills with one man so that we may kill him and all our glory with another so that we may line the streets for him'. With that sardonic equation we may agree, while noting the ironies in his summing up: 'What a nonsense it all is'.

Moon, on the other hand, vacillates between vain attempts to sort things out and more dangerous attempts to obliterate them from awareness. But the deceptive and exploitative conduct of others arouses in him a feverish or frozen alarm with which we must sympathise, and he often suggests how we must move though this book. When he tries to interrogate his wife about her relations with the cowboys, her coy non-sequiturs derail his thought much as the book's structure has been derailing ours: 'Every response gave Moon the feeling that reality was just outside his perception. If he made a certain move, changed the angle of his existence to the common ground, logic and absurdity would separate. As it was he couldn't pin them down'. A moment later his perception is further unsettled by the grotesque appearance of Jane's pink lips and green eyes: 'Once more the commonplace had duped him into seeing absurdity, just as absurdity kept tricking him into accepting it as commonplace'. And much later it occurs to him 'that the labyrinthine riddle of London's streets might be subjected to a single mathematical formula, one of such sophistication that it would relate the whole hopeless mess into a coherent logic'.

Lord Malquist soon offers one formula for those streets as he lectures Moon:

I share your distrust at the way of the world, it is unequal, inadequate and quite without discrimination. But you must learn that the flaw is not an aberration of society but runs right through the structure. Why, this very street is its monument. . . . The Admiralty on one side, the War Office on the other, ever-expanding monoliths disposing a never-diminishing force, at enormous cost and with motives so obscured by time and experience that the sufferings incurred at the further ends can only be ascribed to the tides of history.

He proceeds to comment at length upon the inhumanity and mass self-deception ironically enshrined in Downing Street, the Foreign Office, the Home Office, the Ministry of Defence, New Scotland Yard, the Houses of Parliament, and Westminster Abbey. As he has earlier told

Jane when touring the streets, 'It is necessary to define one's context at all times'.

That is exactly what we must do as we move through the labyrinthine riddle of this book. Unlike its characters, *Lord Malquist and Mr Moon* withdraws from no chaos within its field of vision. It focuses the violence and pain that result from our attempts to repress awareness or eliminate its objects, and it asks us to do much sorting out that is beyond Lord Malquist's taste or Moon's competence. The book's own style, though apparently sceptical and equivocal, encompasses those of its characters by inviting us to play a game that relies on quite firm aesthetic and ethical norms. We might call it 'defining our context.' It assumes that our relish for apparent chaos is greater than our fear of it, that our delight in puzzle-solving can become an instrument of moral awareness, and that our participation in the act of realising a complex artistic form can lead to a salutary meditation upon the self-deceptions and cruelties caused by our anxiety to escape into forms less capacious.

The game begins as Chapter One takes us through six brief sections, each shaped by a different style and point of view. Each section tempts us to posit a different context, or extrapolate from our brief glimpses a different artistic world. First we meet Lord Malquist and Moon in the coach, mediated by a style that conflates the narrator's ironic terseness and Moon's nearly hysterical be-fuddlement. The place is obviously London. And the time? Well, some years after the fall of the Bastille, and after the Battle of Waterloo. But how many? The city traffic is a blur that defies more accurate placement. Only when Lord Malquist, after scattering luminous gold coins about the street, unwraps one and pops the chocolate into his mouth do we fix upon a roughly contemporary date.

(The exact date will surface in our minds much later, after we identify the unnamed national hero). At once, however, we cut to a cowboy who is moseying down an apparently open slope. The narrator's style has now become deceptively like that of some commercial Western tale: 'The things that you noticed were the single gun on his left hip and the tough leather chaps that covered his denims though this wasn't cactus country'. After the cowboy has encountered his rival in love, again we note a suspicious clue: he has not even recognised the sex of the mare he is riding on. Another cut then takes us to what might be North Africa, and to Hemingway's cadences: 'From behind a scrub of thorn the lion watched her. He was not sure yet and the wind was wrong.' But soon the language is corrupted by melodramatic inflation. The approaching woman staggers onward with 'eyes red-rimmed and desperate'. 'Her mouth and throat, her whole body, felt as if she had never taken a drink in her life and all the dry years were compressed now into a terrible need'. After her collapse, another cut takes us to what might be the Near East, and to some simple religious tale. An humble figure on his donkey passes by a small lake, hopes to find a fig tree, sleeps for several hours, and then enters the city – only to provoke a traffic jam, lose his temper, kick the donkey in the genitals, swear at it, and collapse weeping. We are then swept into a pretentious romantic novel:

> Jane was sitting at her toilette, as she called it in the French manner, dreaming of might-have-beens. It was the height of the season in London, and an onlooker might have been forgiven for wondering why it was that this mere slip of a girl with her hair spun like gold, with exquisite features that proclaimed a noble breeding, should sit alone with sadness in her heart.

33

When a cowboy arrives to find Jane sitting on what an American would call the toilet, we are confirmed in our suspicion that these disparate styles and characters must form parts of the same world. But how? Returning us to the coach, the sixth introductory section locates us now in Moon's internal monologue as he reflects upon his own need to order the chaos by means of some explosion.

Stoppard's method here has obvious links with that in Joyce's *Ulysses*. It warns us that every style projects a world, and that beyond the limits of every world we will find not chaos but another world projected by another style, either more or less capacious. It is therefore absurd to try to cope with our discomfort by tossing a bomb or tossing the book away, or by retreating into some habitually preferred style of interpretation and judgement through which, like Lord Malquist or Jane or the Risen Christ, we might seek a knowingly factitious salvation. We must move attentively through a landscape of diverse styles that disclose, even as they deform, an otherwise unknowable reality. Madness, as Moon will later recognise, is 'the ultimate rationalisation of the private view'. Alerted in Chapter One to the disproportions in diction or tone that signal the willed inauthenticity that drives toward madness, we have already begun to wrestle with the question that Moon later asks himself: '*Who's a genuine what*?' And in various ways – for, having made the point, Stoppard can drop the mechanical cutting – the next five chapters test our alertness to action as mediated by style.

In Chapter Two do we forget – as Moon does for thirteen pages – that Marie is still lying frightened, wounded, or worse, under the chesterfield? And are we as surprised as he is to find that O'Hara's face is not, as he had somehow remembered it, 'Irish, boozy, and fat'? In

Chapter Three, can we detect how much Moon has deliberately censored in that Pepysian journal entry which we will (in the next chapter) see him write, after his notebook has been first soaked and then burned 'to its brittle essence'? In Chapter Four, as he reaches his amorous goal, and Laura turns under him with underwater grace and grips hard, 'making sea-moans that lingered in the flooded chambers of his mind', can we hear in Stoppard's submarine sentences the surging of 'The Love Song of J. Alfred Prufrock'? In Chapter Five, do we recognise the stylistic recapitulation of Chapter One as the characters – now clearly puppets of themselves in their own imaginary worlds – approach Trafalgar Square for their final recognitions and reversals? And by the end of Chapter Six, have we realised how this playfully macabre and fertile design has focused the 'brittle essence' of our anxiously conflicting and self-deceptive styles?

Lord Malquist and Mr Moon may be too brittle, too hollow, because it risks disclosing through its stylistic virtuosity our usual lack of substance. But it indicates Stoppard's humane commitments and his faith in our ability to play the game it constitutes. The near absence of humanity within its amusing and alarming world is answered by our discerning presence in that game. A similar paradox is central to the play that made Stoppard's reputation in 1967 while this novel remained virtually unread. Considered as a text, *Rosencrantz and Guildenstern Are Dead* is no less brittle or hollow than *Lord Malquist and Mr Moon* – and much the same might be said of *Jumpers, Travesties,* and the later plays. As plays, however, they are not merely texts but scores for performance. Our participation in their games is therefore of a different order. As actors and witnesses in the theatre, we give body to the worlds they portray and also to our action of exploring them. We fill their forms with our shared presence. On that fact, adumbrated as early as *Enter a Free Man,* Stoppard would base his major work.

3

Playing Our Absence

We are at the Old Vic on an evening in April 1967. As the stage-lights go up, two men dressed as Elizabethan courtiers are tossing coins. The one in a red coat – dark-haired and rather lanky – sits by a nearly empty money bag and spins them high in the air. His partner in a blue coat – blonder and stockier – walks about retrieving them and putting them into a nearly full bag. It is 'heads' every time. Soon the one in red says to nobody in particular, 'There is an art to the building of suspense'. A comment on their game, or on this new play? A bit later he gets up, examines the stage while spinning coins over his shoulder, and speculates that the law of averages 'means that if six monkeys were thrown up in the air for long enough they would land on their tails about as often as they would land on their —' 'Heads,' says his partner, picking up a coin. By the time their run of 'heads' has exceeded eighty-five, the increasingly agitated courtier in red has begun also to spin fantastic syllogisms and hypotheses to account for what is happening.

One hypothesis: 'Inside where nothing shows, I am the essence of a man spinning double-headed coins, and betting against himself in private atonement for an unremembered past'. Another: 'time has stopped dead, and the single experience of one coin being spun once has been repeated ninety times'. Again his remarks have an odd applicability to the play we are watching. The courtiers themselves are rather like two sides of some double-headed coin, and nothing they have said thus far tells us who is who. Our programmes, of course, list John Stride as Rosencrantz and Edward Petherbridge as Guildenstern in the National Theatre Company's production of this new play (directed by Derek Goldby, designed by Dennis Heeley, with lighting by Richard Pilbrow), and some of us are quite sure that the lankier and more eloquent courtier in red must be Petherbridge and therefore Guildenstern – but others are not. And the characters are of no help at all, for they have only the foggiest notion of their past, their future, and their present whereabouts. Sometimes they speak almost like members of the audience suddenly transported to the stage. 'We were sent for,' says the stockier one in blue, who must be Stride and therefore Rosencrantz. 'Yes,' says Petherbridge. 'That's why we're here,' says Stride, looking about them as if he doubted his own assertion. 'Travelling.' Indeed, they may be too late – but for what? 'How do I know? We haven't got there yet.' 'Then what are we doing here, I ask myself,' says Petherbridge, as if he were both of them. 'You might well ask,' says Stride. 'We better get on,' says Petherbridge. 'You might well think,' says Stride. 'We better get on,' says Petherbridge again, as if for all of us.

What *are* they doing, and *where*? Are they in *Hamlet*? Or just outside it? Or in an outrageously impossible world?

Or in our own time? Or inside our assembled heads where nothing shows? Or in the timeless land of the dead, where a single experience repeats itself endlessly? Or in the open space where Beckett's Vladimir and Estragon wait for Godot? Or the closed space where his Hamm and Clov are always 'getting on'? Or in a self-parodic play on the empty stage of the Old Vic? The answer, we will discover, is 'all of the above'. From moment to moment as the play proceeds, all of those frames of reference will be moving in and out of focus. And even after we think we know who is who – a point on which Rosencrantz and Guildenstern themselves will never reach final clarity – we will be puzzled to say what is really taking place. From one point of view our spectatorial protagonists will seem as free as we are: they will struggle to understand their predicament, respond to it sometimes with astonishing verbal resourcefulness, repeatedly break out of the plot of *Hamlet*, manage to rationalise or repress their betrayal of its hero, and finally choose to make no effort to escape their doom. And yet they are obviously marked for death, subject to a fate that is doubly or triply 'written': in *Hamlet*, in Stoppard's own script, and perhaps in the dim cosmic order that includes all human scripts. And yet again, the working out of that fate is most whimsical and improbable, an evident sign of Stoppard's own spontaneous play with *Hamlet*, *Waiting for Godot*, half a dozen other scripts, and the main assumptions of modern culture. We will not be able to reduce such contradictions to a logically consistent 'imitation' or 'representation' of life. Here, as in modern physics, a thinking based on the law of the excluded middle can have no final authority. To describe the world in *Rosencrantz and Guildenstern Are Dead* we would need something like Niels Bohr's notion of complementary explanations, according to which opposite concepts have meaning only in terms of their participation in each other.

But even that would not be enough, for the meaning of this play is not confined to its 'represented world'. *Rosencrantz and Guildenstern Are Dead* is shaped by a recognition that dramatic meaning always inheres in our present acting and witnessing of represented events. Its own full meaning therefore inheres in our acting and witnessing of a contradictory pseudo-representation that acknowledges our presence in the theatre. When Graham Crowden enters as the Player (a self-assured and sardonic master of the melodramatic school, wearing a tattered and beribboned suit with a paisley-print jerkin, and accompanied by a seedy troupe of Tragedians), he uses a now familiar metaphor and an ancient but up-to-date theatrical allusion to make that point clear – to us if not to Rosencrantz and Guildenstern. He recognises them, he says rather effusively, as 'fellow artists'. Why? 'For some of us it is performance, for others patronage. They are two sides of the same coin, or let us say, being as there are so many of us, the same side of two coins.' He bows deeply and then adds, refurbishing a line from Archie Rice's (or was it Laurence Olivier's?) last sad music-hall performance in John Osborne's *The Entertainer*: 'Don't clap too loudly – it's a very old world.'

But as 'fellow artists', participants in a play that anticipates *Lord Malquist and Mr Moon* in casting the 'spectator as hero', who are we? We think we know, as long as nobody asks us – and our commonsense belief in our determinate identity seems to provide a comfortable basis for our enjoyment of the play's own indeterminacy. But if we put the question to ourselves quite seriously, we must confess our ignorance. Humanity in our time has become problematic or unfindable. Philosophers since Nietzsche and dramatists since Ibsen have stripped us of mask after mask. God is dead; the soul is an outdated fiction. Physicists, chemists, and biologists investigate fields of energy that nothing directs. Psychologists and sociologists analyse roles that no one performs. Inside, 'where nothing shows', we suspect that our subjectivity is a mechanical result of unknown causes, and that language is a self-elaborating process without reference. In an absurd void like that of Beckett's *Endgame*, 'Something is taking its course'. How then can 'we' be 'here' at all?

Rosencrantz and Guildenstern Are Dead invites us to play with that anxious question. Its title proclaims the effective absence of its protagonists from our historical moment, their own play, and life itself. Like Vladimir and Estragon in *Waiting for Godot*, they are uncertain of their identity and their destiny. Though Guildenstern seems more intelligent than Rosencrantz, they cannot even keep their own names straight. 'Give us this day our daily mask', says Guildenstern – but not to any deity. 'What are you playing at?' asks Rosencrantz. 'Words, words,' replies Guildenstern, echoing Vladimir, who echoed Hamlet. 'They're all we have to go on.' Lacking any firm criteria for probability, evidence, logic, or sanity, they meet no one who is much better equipped. The Player tells them that 'truth is only that which is taken to be true. It's the currency of living. There may be nothing behind it, but it doesn't make any difference so long as it's honoured. One acts on assumptions.' Rosencrantz assumes that 'Hamlet is not himself, outside or in.' And for the Player and his troupe the single assumption that makes 'existence viable' is that 'somebody is *watching*.' Otherwise they are 'stripped naked in the middle of nowhere' and pouring themselves 'down a bottomless well.'

For Rosencrantz and Guildenstern, in fact, the only available truth seems a currency of death. Unlike Vladimir and Estragon, they are already part of what the Player will call the 'design' of tragedy, in which 'everyone who is marked for death dies.' In *Waiting for Godot* there is nearly always an 'even chance' with respect to anything at all, but here Rosencrantz and Guildenstern start off in the midst of an improbable and ominous run of 'heads' that will end just at the moment when they intersect with the script of *Hamlet*. In Act Two, Guildenstern accommodates himself to the suspicion that they are part of a larger order:

> Wheels have been set in motion, and they have their own pace, to which we are . . . condemned. Each move is dictated by the previous one – that is the meaning of order. If we start being arbitrary it'll just be a shambles: at least, let us hope so. Because if we happened, just happened to discover, or even suspect, that our spontaneity was part of their order, we'd know that we were lost.

When the players rehearse their dumbshow, it continues through the poisoning of the Player-King and the main events of *Hamlet* to the deaths of the two smiling spies who have escorted the Prince to England. Though almost recognising that the spies wear coats identical to their own, Rosencrantz and Guildenstern fail to perceive the order of which their spontaneity must be a part. In Act Three, finding themselves on a boat for England with a letter that decrees the death of Hamlet, they relax into what Guildenstern thinks a limited freedom: 'Spontaneity and whim are the order of the day. Other wheels are turning but they are not our concern'. And after the pirate attack, Guildenstern seems resigned to their destiny: 'We've travelled too far, and our momentum has taken over; we move idly towards eternity, without possibility of reprieve or hope of explanation'. But for us their destiny is a 'dead end' that seems to express the entire meaning of their so-called life from the moment of their summons to the stage. Perhaps the main achievement of Vladimir and Estragon in *Waiting for Godot* is their persistence in 'being there'. But in this respect Rosencrantz and Guildenstern are rather more like *Endgame*'s Hamm and Clov: they are chronically absent from their own lives. 'I say to myself – sometimes,' says Clov, '. . . you must be there better than that if you want them to let you go – one day.' And Hamm says: 'Absent always. It all happened without me. I don't know what's happened'. As Stoppard's pair now drift toward death, Guildenstern will say: 'Death is not anything . . . death is not . . . It's the absence of presence, nothing more . . . .' And both of them will suddenly disappear, quite as if they had never been here at all.

Charles Marowitz spoke for a good many reviewers of the 1967 production in London when he called this play 'an existential comedy whose ur-text . . . is *En Attendant Godot*' and praised Stoppard's 'remarkable skill in juggling the *données* of existential philosophy'. But Stoppard himself later disclaimed any intention of engaging that philosophy. Nine years after writing the play, he said (in 'Ambushes for the Audience: Toward a High Comedy of Ideas') that his conscious calculation had been wholly on the problem of how 'to entertain a roomful of people' by constructing 'a series of small, large, and microscopic ambushes' – verbal and theatrical surprises. And what of existentialism? 'First I must say that I didn't know what the word 'existential ' meant until it was applied to *Rosencrantz*. And even now existentialism is not a philosophy I find either attractive or plausible.' Though granting that 'the play can be interpreted in existential terms, as well as in other terms', he insisted that he had proceeded here, as in later plays, by 'a sort of infinite leap-frog' through 'a series of conflicting statements by conflicting characters'. 'You know, an argument, a refutation, then a rebuttal of the refutation, then a counter-rebuttal, so that there is never any point in this intellectual leap-frog at which I feel *that* is a speech to stop it on, *that* is the last word.' In *Lord Malquist and Mr Moon* the baffled Moon had spoken in just those terms of leapfrogging himself along the great moral issues. Though overwhelmed by uncertainty, Moon too might have denied knowing what is meant by 'existential'. And what if we had given him Sartre's *Nausea, Being and Nothingness,* and *No Exit* to read? Even though Moon's visions of the 'remorseless uncontrollable, unguided growth' or 'monstrous spawn' in the London streets seem very much like that which afflicts Roquentin in *Nausea* – or else precisely because they are symptoms of the same hysteria – he too might easily have retorted that he finds existentialism neither 'attractive' nor 'plausible'.

It is likely, therefore, that Stoppard's response was both accurate and slightly misleading. In fact, there are some striking similarities between the situation of Rosencrantz and Guildenstern and that of Sartre's already dead characters in *No Exit*. The boat in Act Three is as ambiguous a confinement as the closed room that constitutes Sartre's hell. Waking there in darkness, Rosencrantz and Guildenstern speculate on their whereabouts. 'We might as well be dead,' says Rosencrantz. 'Do you think death could possibly be a boat?' Like Sartre's Inez, Garcin, and Estelle, whose *post mortem* state eternalises their evasion of existential presence, they indulge themselves now in what seems a trivial freedom without risk. And just as Sartre's characters insist on remaining in the room even when the door flies open, never really challenging the impersonal 'design' of which Inez speaks, so Rosencrantz and Guildenstern never challenge the deathly 'design' of which the Player speaks – even though Stoppard, unlike Shakespeare, lets them discover the contents of both Claudius' letter and that which Hamlet puts in its place. The climax of *No Exit* is a pathetic and farcical attempt to murder the dead. In a fit of jealousy, Estelle knifes Inez, who cries out: 'Knives, poison, ropes – all useless. It has happened *already,* do you understand? Once and for all. So here we are, forever'. The analogous climax of *Rosencrantz and Guildenstern Are Dead* is the anguished Guildenstern's attempt to knife the Player – who then rises from his momentarily convincing death, reveals the knife to be collapsible, and orders his troupe to demonstrate 'Deaths by suspension, convulsion, consumption, incision, execution, asphyxiation and malnutrition –! Climactic carnage, by poison and by steel –!' Surely we want to cry out to Rosencrantz and Guildenstern: 'It has happened *already*, do you understand? So there you are, forever'. But where? Dead, or in a most paradoxical play?

No Exit does not need to burden itself with the word 'existentialism', but the British play that seems most immediately behind *Rosencrantz and Guildenstern Are Dead* is more explicit about its philosophical bearings. James Saunders' *Next Time I'll Sing to You* had received some very favourable attention in London in 1963. Saunders himself was one of the playwrights with whom Stoppard went to West Berlin in the following year. And it was Saunders who urged Stoppard to expand his verse burlesque, *Rosencrantz and Guildenstern Meet King Lear,* into a full-length play. In *Next Time I'll Sing to You* a writer named Rudge insists on the significance of a Hermit who spent his life isolated amid 'being and nonbeing'. 'The point is,' says Rudge, 'he *existed.* Beneath an empty sky.' One of Rudge's companions elsewhere retorts to such insistence:'I'm not going to bandy existentialism with you'. And perhaps for good reason. Rudge himself has 'written' the play in which they all appear. No character has any existence except as a role 'written' by one whose identity, behind his own self-designed role, remains unknown. But if the absence of these characters is as evident as their loquacious presence, it does not follow that Saunders' play expounds or refutes existentialism. It is one thing to declare a philosophical position and another to toss us a question that has charged our intellectual climate and ask us to play with it.

The idiosyncratic playfulness of *Rosencrantz and Guildenstern Are Dead* has, in fact, a complex ancestry. To track it down is to begin to see how this script variously probes an absence that seems always already 'written'. Its interrelated themes of appearance and reality, sanity and insanity, and presence and absence are broached, of course, in *Hamlet* itself, as the opening lines of that play suggest: 'Who's there?' ''Nay, answer me. Stand, and unfold yourself.' Bernardo and Francisco on the battlements might for a moment almost be Stoppard's Rosencrantz and Guildenstern bandying unanswerable questions. We soon learn that an already dead king will set this plot in motion. His son, shunted to the periphery of the royal scene, where he holds forth in problematic soliloquies, first claims to have 'that within which passeth show', then says he will 'put an antic disposition on', and then proceeds to behave with such outrageous ambiguity that Polonius thinks him mad, Claudius thinks him shamming, and countless viewers of his tragedy will be unable to distinguish between his haunted sanity and his lucid madness. To this distraught man, subjective relativity is already a problem, 'for there is nothing either good or bad, but thinking makes it so'. The world for him is a goodly prison; books contain nothing but 'Words, words, words'; and the overwhelming question is whether 'To be or not to be'. Hamlet's much too affable schoolfellows, summoned to search out his affliction, soon find themselves escorting him to England, the unwitting bearers of a letter that decrees his death. Thanks to Hamlet's own devices, that death will become their own. 'So Guildenstern and Rosencrantz go to 't,' says Horatio, when Hamlet recounts the tale. And Hamlet replies with what may seem callous detachment:

> Why, man, they did make love to this employment.
> They are not near my conscience; their defeat
> Does by their own insinuation grow.
> 'Tis dangerous when the baser nature comes
> Between the pass and fell incensèd points
> Of mighty opposites.

But of course a man's life, for Hamlet, is now 'no more than to say "one"', a brief absence from felicity.

Recapitulating by deliberate design or spontaneous affinity a fair number of post-Shakespearean developments, *Rosencrantz and Guildenstern Are Dead* manages to turn *Hamlet* inside out. It shunts the entire tragedy to the periphery of the theatrical scene, where we glimpse it through bits of Shakespearean dialogue and accelerated mime. As the plot of *Hamlet* becomes a dimly apprehended 'infernal machine', rather like that which propels Oedipus' life in Jean Cocteau's play of that name, our 'baser nature' becomes the object of our attention and

47

concern. Hamlet's schoolfellows, those self-styled 'indifferent children of the earth', become our own fellows, lively Prufrocks – attendant lords, easy tools, deferential, glad to be of use, 'Full of high sentence, but a bit obtuse' – who rehearse their overwhelming questions as tney seek roles in a play that has already written them down as dead. A step toward that reversal of perspective had been taken by W. S. Gilbert's verse burlesque of 1874, *Rosencrantz and Guildenstern*, which produces some wry shifts in sympathy as it deflates Shakespearean rhetoric. Stoppard's own verse burlesque of 1964 may have had a similar emphasis. Charles Marowitz, who was an adjudicator at the Berlin colloquium, thought *Rosencrantz and Guildenstern Meet King Lear* 'a lot of academic twaddle'. Martin Esslin, another adjudicator, has recalled that Rosencrantz and Guildenstern, on landing at Dover, meet the mad Lear crying 'Kill, kill, kill, kill, kill' – and are killed. In any case, the National Theatre Company appropriately included excerpts from Gilbert's burlesque in its programme for Stoppard's revised and expanded play in 1967.

According to Gilbert, Gertrude has sent for the pair to search out the cause of Hamlet's soliloquising and distract him with court revels. Ophelia, who is here Rosencrantz's former love, tells them that:

> The favourite theory's somewhat like this:
> Hamlet is idiotically sane
> With lucid intervals of lunacy.

(When Stoppard's pair diagnose Hamlet's soliloquising, they conclude that a man who talks sense to himself and nonsense not to himself must be 'Stark raving sane'.) Hoping to prevent Ophelia's marriage, Rosencrantz joins with her to persuade Hamlet to perform a bombastic tragedy, 'Gonzago', which had been written by Claudius in his youth, laughed off the stage, and then decreed unmentionable on pain of death. Hamlet, ignorant of the play's authorship and proscription, performs its main role in Gilbertian style: 'For I hold that there is no such antick fellow as your bombastical hero who doth so earnestly spout forth his folly as to make his hearers believe that he is unconscious of all incongruity'. He escapes the death penalty but is banished to England, where his 'philosophic brain' may be appreciated, and Rosencrantz wins back Ophelia.

During a soliloquy that Rosencrantz and Guildenstern try to interrupt, Gilbert's burlesque comes fairly close to the verbal texture of Stoppard's play:

HAM.: To be – or not to be!

ROS.: Yes – that's the question –
   Whether he's bravest who will cut his throat
   Rather than suffer all –

GUILD.: Or suffer all
   Rather than cut his throat?

HAM.: [*annoyed at interruption, says* 'Go away – go away!' *then resumes*]: To die – to sleep –

ROS.: It's nothing more – Death is but sleep spun out –
   Why hesitate? [*Offers him a dagger*]

GUILD.: The only question is
   Between the choice of deaths, which death to choose.
[*Offers a revolver*]

HAM.: [*in great terror*]: Do take those dreadful things away. They make
   My blood run cold. Go away – go away! [*They turn aside.*

HAMLET *resumes*] To sleep, perchance to –

ROS.: Dream.
    That's very true. I never dream myself,
    But Guildenstern dreams all night long out loud.

GUILD. [*coming down and kneeling*]: With blushes, sir, I
    do confess it true!

HAM.: This question, gentlemen, concerns me not.
    [*Resumes*] For who would bear the whips and scorns
    of time –

ROS. [*as guessing a riddle*]: *Who'd* bear the whips
    and scorns? Now, let me see.
    Who'd *bear* them, eh?

GUILD. [*same business*]: Who'd bear the *scorns* of time?

ROS. [*correcting him*]: The *whips* and scorns.

GUILD.: The whips and scorns, of course.

[HAMLET *about to protest*]
    Don't tell us – let us guess – the *whips* of time?

HAM.: Oh, sirs, this interruption likes us not.
    I pray you give it up.

ROS.: My lord, we do.
    We cannot tell *who* bears these whips and scorns.

HAM. [*not heeding them, resumes*]: But that the dread
    of something *after* death –

ROS.: That's true – *post mortem* and the coroner –
    Felo de se – cross roads at twelve P.M. –
    And then the forfeited life policy –
    Exceedingly unpleasant.

HAM. [*really angry*]: Gentlemen,
    It must be patent to the merest dunce
    Three persons can't soliloquise at once!

In revising and expanding his own verse play, Stoppard presented that soliloquy as a mime, with comments by Rosencrantz and Guildenstern from the sidelines, but he also wrote for his protagonists a great deal of joint-soliloquising in the form of witty prose duets that draw upon the work of two of Gilbert's lineal descendants, Wilde and Beckett. It is almost as though Vladimir and Estragon, tired of waiting for Godot, had donned Elizabethan costume, acquired something of the absurd elegance of Algernon Moncrieff and John Worthing in *The Importance of Being Earnest*, and journeyed to the Danish court. As Kenneth Tynan has noted, Wilde himself in *De Profundis* had praised Shakespeare's subtle portrayal of characters who are so close to Hamlet's secret but know nothing of it:

> Nor would there be any use in telling them. They are little cups that can hold so much and no more. . . . They are types fixed for all time. To censure them would show a lack of appreciation. They are merely out of their sphere: that is all.

Stoppard's types inherit from Beckett's their uncertainty, failing memory, and confused identity, as well as their music-hall routines, verbal game-playing, and pointed use of such phrases as 'Words, words', 'I forget', 'It's the normal thing', and 'I'm going'. Both pairs at times seem hardly more than functions of a language that proceeds by self-contradiction or self-cancellation. Beckett had achieved through stichomythic exchanges a wide range of effects, from low comedy and sardonic wit to an echoing lyricism. The usually lighter and swifter exchanges between Rosencrantz and Guildenstern run from banal repetition to high fooling, witty debates invaded by hysteria, and such skilful incompetence as appears when they role-play their interrogation of Hamlet:

> ROS.: Let me get it straight. Your father was king. You were his only son. Your father dies. You are of age. Your uncle becomes king.

GUIL.: Yes.
ROS.: Unorthodox.
GUIL.: Undid me.
ROS.: Undeniable. Where were you?
GUIL.: In Germany.
ROS.: Usurpation, then.
GUIL.: He slipped in.
ROS.: Which reminds me.
GUIL.: Well, it would.
ROS.: I don't want to be personal.
GUIL.: It's common knowledge.
ROS:: Your mother's marriage.
GUIL.: He slipped in.
   [*Beat*]

Unlike Beckett's characters, however, Stoppard's can take longer rhetorical flights. When Guildenstern holds forth on the law of probability ('The scientific approach to the examination of phenomena is a defence against the pure emotion of fear') or the nature of evidence (' ''The colours red, blue and green are real. The colour yellow is a mystical experience shared by everybody'' – demolish'), Wilde's Algy and Jack might admire his elegance and aplomb. When he speaks of the summons in quasi-Faulknerian terms, of course, they might be baffled:

All your life you live so close to truth, it becomes a permanent blur in the corner of your eye, and when something nudges it into outline it is like being ambushed by a grotesque. A man standing in his saddle in the half-lit half-alive dawn banged on the shutters and called two names. He was just a hat and a cloak levitating in the grey plume of his own breath, but when he called we came. That much is certain – we came.

Those self-possessed but edgy young men so hot for a christening would soon recognise home ground, however, in a Wildean exchange that also seems to glance at Eliot's 'Journey of the Magi' ('were we led all that way for/Birth or Death?'):

> ROS.: Well I can tell you I'm sick to death of it. I don't care one way or another, so why don't you make up your mind.
> GUIL: We can't afford anything quite so arbitrary. Nor did we come all this way for a christening. All *that* – preceded us. But we are comparatively fortunate; we might have been left to sift the whole field of human nomenclature, like two blind men looting a bazaar for their own portraits.

Even the duller but more sensitive Rosencrantz can express the emotional centre of their predicament with a literate eloquence, though no doubt unaware that he is rebutting both Hemingway's 'Indian Camp' and Wordsworth's 'Intimations of Immortality':

> What ever became of the moment when one first knew about death? There must have been one, a moment, in childhood when it first occurred to you that you don't go on for ever. It must have been shattering – stamped into one's memory. And yet I can't remember it. It never occurred to me at all. What does one make of that? We must be born with an intuition of mortality. Before we know the words for it, before we know that there are words, out we come, bloodied and squalling with the knowledge that for all the compasses in the world, there's only one direction, and time is its only measure.

Despite such moments of anguished presence to their own predicament, Rosencrantz and Guildenstern are chronically 'not there'. In developing that trait – which is endemic in the Hamlet tradition from the Prince himself down to Chekhov's Vanya, Joyce's Stephen Dedalus, Pirandello's nameless man who plays Enrico IV, and Beckett's Hamm – Stoppard has come close to yet other explorations of histrionic absence. In Pirandello's *Six Characters in Search of an Author*, the visitors who want to stage their aborted story are fixed for all time as incompletely realised 'characters' but are also movingly 'real' as they debate the meaning of their roles. Conversely, the actors to whom they appear are ostensibly 'real' but quite obviously stage types, unable to approach the reality of the offered story. Though Stoppard later told Giles Gordon that he knew 'very little' about Pirandello, he effectively complicated Pirandello's dialectic between art and life by having his yet more confused 'characters' meet an 'actor' who is both a philosopher and a personification of role-playing.

The Player's assertion that 'actors' are 'the opposite of people' twists the Pirandellian definition of 'characters' to emphasise not fixity but an empty theatricality. A moral relativist for whom any sustained appearance is indistinguishable from reality, the Player also sounds like some dandy or double-dealer in one of the Restoration comedies admired by Wilde and echoed by Lord Malquist. In fact, his paradoxical rhetoric often suggests Wilde's, and on one occasion he wittily revises *The Importance of Being Earnest*. Speaking of the novel she had written as a young woman, Miss Prism tells her pupil Cecily: 'The good ended happily, and the bad unhappily. That is what Fiction means'. Instructing Rosencrantz and Guildenstern in the design of an art in which everything is already 'written,' the Player says: 'We follow directions – there is no *choice* involved. The bad end unhappily, the good unluckily. That is what tragedy means'. As one who thinks he exists only when somebody is watching, he also recalls the characters in Sartre's *No Exit*, who require the mirroring gaze of others. But as a leering decadent who justifies his troupe's homosexual rites with a sardonic nihilism, he suggests the playwright most celebrated by Sartre. When the Court Envoy in Genet's *The Balcony* expounds the mysteries of 'absence' represented by the 'infinite meditation' of the 'unfindable' Queen, he says: 'I mean that the Queen is embroidering and that she is not embroidering. She picks her nose, examines the pickings and lies down again. Then she dries the dishes'. Stoppard's Player, coarsely demystifying such mysteries as he expounds them, rebukes the young actor who plays the Queen in Stoppard's version of 'The Murder of Gonzago': 'Stop picking your nose, Alfred. When Queens have to they do it by a cerebral process passed down in the blood'. (Lord Malquist would soon embroider that line further: 'You probably know that the Malquists in common with other families of equal style and breeding excrete and procreate by a cerebral process the secret of which is passed down in the blood'.)

Two phrases used by Rosencrantz were also already 'written' in Edward Albee's *The Zoo Story,* where a conversation in the existential void of Central Park begins with talk about geography. 'Have I been walking north?' asks Jerry. When Peter confirms that disingenuous speculation, Jerry says: 'Good old north'. And then: 'But not due north'. Peter stammers a bit and settles for this: 'It's northerly'. In Stoppard's play, an echo of that conversation combines with a more explicit allusion to Hamlet's ability to know a hawk from a handsaw 'when

the wind is southerly' and some self-conscious theatricality from *Waiting for Godot* to suggest the impossibility
of any orientation:

> ROS.: . . . [*Licks his finger and holds it up – facing
> audience*]:
> Is that southerly?
> [*They stare at audience*]
> GUIL.: It doesn't *look* southerly. What made you think
> so?
> ROS.: I didn't *say* I think so. It could be northerly for
> all I know.

Later on, Rosencrantz decides that the audience must be to
the east: 'I think we can assume that'. 'I'm assuming
nothing,' retorts Guildenstern. But Rosencrantz persists:
'Good old east'.

Of special importance to Stoppard, however, must have
been Saunders' very recent exploration of histrionic
absence, *Next Time I'll Sing to You*. Certainly it relieved
him of the need to know more than 'very little' about
Pirandello, for it has already combined the predicaments
of *Waiting for Godot* and *No Exit* with that of *Six
Characters in Search of an Author*. In a script that alludes
to its own nightly repetition, the characters, actors,
author, and spectators are interchangeable aspects of a
single situation. Lizzie, who stands in on alternate nights
for her sister Lizzie, insists: 'I want to know what I *am*'.
'And what special virtue do you think you possess,' asks
Rudge, who has written the script that contains him, 'that
you should be granted this piece of knowledge denied to
the rest of us?' Addressing the actor who plays the already
dead Hermit, Dust expands on their plight: 'You have a
part to play and naturally you wish to know what is the

part and what is the essential you which is playing the part. So do they, of course,' he adds, pointing to the audience. 'That's what they're sitting there for.'

Though Rudge wants 'to understand the purpose of existence', he can only affirm the disconcertingly unreal. Saunders' maundering and fitfully eloquent play, however, is a useful compendium of ways in which a playwright can focus our interchangeable roles. And one whimsical passage of verbal cricket seems to have been of yet more specific help:

RUDGE: . . . Right, I'll open the bowling . . .
MEFF: Play!
RUDGE: Right. Ladies and gentlemen, we crave –
MEFF: No ball!
RUDGE: Ladies and gentlemen –
MEFF: No ball.
RUDGE: What is our purpose here tonight?
DUST: Don't ask them, *tell* them.
RUDGE: The question's rhetorical.
MEFF: No ball.
RUDGE: Why not?
MEFF: Rule Fifteen. The bowling of rhetorical questions, rhymed cutlets or four-letter words either overarm or underarm shall constitute a no-ball in the sense aforementioned.

Changing the cricket to tennis, Stoppard came up with a more ingenious and rapid-fire game in which every shot must be a question, and all statements, repetitions, grunts, synonyms, and rhetorical questions are grounds for calling 'Foul!'

Such playfulness is the very centre of *Rosencrantz and Guildenstern Are Dead,* utterly transforming its characters and themes. That is why some critics have complained of a lack of authentic despair in its echoes of alienation, scepticism, and nihilism, and why others have offered such conflicting accounts of its method and meaning. Charles Marowitz was right in saying that the 'originality' of this play 'does not lie in its thought, but in its craft'. But he was surely wrong to suggest that the craft finally leaves us with 'a blinding metaphor about the absurdity of life'. Disagreeing with that kind of assessment, Ruby Cohn called the play a 'witty commentary' without integral relation to its Hamlet scenes and Godot situation. The play's primary mode, however, is neither metaphor nor commentary, though it uses both, but a dramatic action that involves all of the participants in the theatrical event. No less concerned with stylistic counterpoint than *Lord Malquist and Mr Moon,* it invites us to play leapfrog with an 'absence' that is always already 'written' – and so rediscover our own presence in the theatre.

The playful dialectic of *Rosencrantz and Guildenstern Are Dead* bases itself on the reciprocal relations among the roles of spectator, actor, character and author. Each imperfectly includes the others. A spectator, for example, is but an implicit actor; an actor can never fully realise his character; a character cannot really become his own author; and even an author is but a spectator of the action he creates. But each role also has its own advantages. Even a character can do much that is beyond the power of an author; an actor can know a freedom beyond that of his characters; and a spectator transcends the limits of all action. In asking us to leapfrog ourselves through these roles, Stoppard clarifies the rather muddled recognition in *Next Time I'll Sing to You* that all are aspects of a single predicament and a single opportunity. Our momentary role may seem impotent and empty – a mere absence from a life that it can never quite grasp. But by entering all roles with lively detachment, we discover our presence in a transpersonal field of play.

As we act or witness *Rosencrantz and Guildenstern Are Dead,* we find ourselves mirrored by its protagonists and drawn with them into an action that traps us by its metaphorical implications. Rosencrantz and Guildenstern first seem ignorant spectators who are trying to enter an as yet undiscovered play. Engaging the plot of *Hamlet,* they begin to seem bad actors who are trying to understand their roles. When they have almost locked themselves into their destiny, they seem to become partial authors of their fate by choosing death. Each step in that ironic progress is a drastic self-limitation. As Guildenstern will finally comment, 'There must have been a moment, at the beginning, where we could have said – no. But somehow we missed it'. And are not we ourselves quite possibly just such characters, following an imperfectly known 'script' that gives us only the choice to die?

But there is another side to this coin. As lively reflectors upon their destiny, Rosencrantz and Guildenstern are bound neither by Shakespeare's plot nor by our usual dullness of speech and imagination. To the very end, they are able to rise into a spectatorial freedom and a quasi-authorial creativity. They may remind us of Walter Benjamin's statement that, in tragedy, fate entails neither a 'causal' nor a 'magical' necessity but evokes 'the unarticulated necessity of defiance in which the self brings forth its utterances'. As actors and witnesses of this play, we share Stoppard's comic version of such a neccessity. Mirrored not merely by the protagonists but also by the play *as* a play – the parodic and self-parodic action that is Stoppard's own response to our already 'written' scripts –

we maintain our spectatorial freedom and move repeatedly towards the condition of author. In effect, our ostensibly prior 'fate' is the condition of our present collaborative freedom. Though the events performed on stage undermine our self-confidence, elicit an anxious recognition of our uncertain identity, and confront us with death, the action of performance invites us to leapfrog through our reciprocal roles toward a playful detachment from such problems.

The play's scenic organisation and stylistic counterpoint shape for us that double movement. Act One begins by using the self-parodic reminiscence of Beckett to explore our relations to spectatorial characters who seem both inside and outside their own play. When they meet the Player, we experience a dialectical clash of both roles and styles, for the Player's self-conscious theatricality requires from the actor who plays him a much more broadly ironic stylisation. Our implicit dialogue with the characters now becomes more fully a dialogue with the play itself. We are prepared to understand the larger meaning of the Player's remark to Rosencrantz and Guildenstern about performers and patrons being flip sides of the same coin. In those spectatorial characters and this self-parodic actor we discover two quite differently distorting mirrors of ourselves and of this play. After the Player's statement that 'It costs little to watch, and little more if you happen to get caught up in the action', and after the tossing of 'tails' has warned us that we will now see the flip side of the plot itself, a third parodic style complicates this dialectic. The lights change: Rosencrantz and Guildenstern freeze; Hamlet chases Ophelia on-stage and mimes the actions that Ophelia recounts to Polonius in Act 2, scene 1, of *Hamlet*; and we are catapulted with our protagonists into the first fifty lines of Act 2, scene 2, of that play. As

Claudius and Gertrude welcome them, we hear Shakespeare's words for the first time – but uttered by characters who seem puzzling travesties of his intention. Reviewing the New York production of 1967 that Derek Goldby also directed, John Chapman remarked that 'As Hamlet, Noel Craig looks like a cadaverous lunatic'. And Martin Gottfried deplored the decision to make 'the actual *Hamlet* scenes so foolish (everybody is played as though by tacky, melodramatic actors)'. But such effects are invited by a script that systematically alienates us from our habitual responses to Shakespeare's tragedy. When most 'inside' that play-within-our-play, we must also be most 'outside' it. Indeed, when Rosencrantz and Guildenstern emerge from that Shakespearean scene, they seem yet more emphatically with us. 'I feel like a spectator,' says Rosencrantz. And Guildenstern, standing at the footlights, remarks: 'What a fine persecution – to be kept intrigued without ever quite being enlightened'. But at once their rapid-fire game of 'questions' again shifts our mental perspective, for it is a remarkable cadenza on the theme of the 'unanswerable' – a theatrical effect that sweeps characters and spectators into a playfully authorial understanding of the action. During this first act we have been put through a lively juggling of such perspectives; and when Rosencrantz and Guildenstern, standing in the two downstage corners, call to a Hamlet who enters upstage, walking backward, the act can end with a lightly comic meeting that holds those perspectives in momentary suspension.

The first intelligible line in Act Two – Hamlet's comment on his own situation in Shakespeare's Act 2, scene 2 – reminds us of the theatrical playfulness in which we are engaged: 'S'blood, there is something in this more than natural, if philosophy could find it out'. By the time we meet the Player again, we sense more clearly the distance between his self-conscious emptiness and Stoppard's kaleidoscopic plenitude. 'One acts on assumptions, he says. But surely the major assumption of this theatrical event is not that we are alienated victims of life's absurdity but that we have the playful ability to call into existence just such an illusion. That point is underlined by 'The Murder of Gonzago' as now performed by the Tragedians for Rosencrantz and Guildenstern – and by Stoppard for us – which recapitulates the entire plot of *Hamlet* and discloses to us the fate of its two uncomprehending spectators, Rosencrantz and Guildenstern. 'Traitors hoist by their own petard? – or victims of the gods? – we shall never know.' For us this play-within-the-play-within-our play is also a beautifully fluid, grotesque, and surprising miming of a tale we think we know, interrupted by a hysterically melodramatic scene between Hamlet and Ophelia that constitutes another version of that tale, and concluded by the quite realistic rendering of Rosencrantz and Guildenstern's half-conscious refusals to recognise here their own images. 'I want a good story, with a beginning, middle and end,' Rosencrantz has said. And Guildenstern has added, 'I'd prefer art to mirror life, if it's all the same to you'. We have now had both, and in several different ways, through a stylistic counterpoint that enacts our own free play with Shakespeare's script. From here on, Act Two will have an increasingly autumnal chill as our protagonists prepare to leave for England. But its final line will sum up both their ironically closed future and our playfully open possibilities: 'And besides,' says Rosencrantz, 'anything could happen yet.'

And almost anything does. For the protagonists, Act Three is an evasive drift toward absence on a boat of death.

For us, however, it is a surprising celebration of theatrical presence. Almost the entire act is a free-floating departure from Shakespeare's script – in effect, a bodying forth of the gap in the main action between Hamlet's leaving for England (Act 4, scene 4) and Horatio's receipt of his letter (Act 4, scene 6). And this death-laden departure from Shakespeare is filled with theatre games that emphasise our possible control over the images of absence. If Rosencrantz and Guildenstern themselves seem yet more clearly puppets – 'Free to move, speak, extemporise, and yet. We have not been cut loose' – they are puppets of the theatre itself. The three large man-sized casks on the deck, the gaudy striped umbrella behind them, and the theatre lights are here the implements of a witty illusionism that will become increasingly dominant. Half-way into the act, Hamlet emerges from behind that umbrella, blows out the light, and switches the letters in Guildenstern's pocket. When the lights come up again, Rosencrantz and Guildenstern hear the muffled sound of a recorder, then a drum, and then a flute (the music of the Tragedians, which has become for us in previous acts a leit-motif of the self-consciously histrionic), and finally discover that the entire band must be in the three barrels. No sooner have the Tragedians piled out, rather like a troupe of clowns emerging from three Volkswagens, than the Pirates attack, whereupon Hamlet leaps into the left-hand barrel, the Player leaps into the right-hand barrel, and Rosencrantz and Guildenstern leap into the middle barrel. The lights dim again to nothing; and when they come up again the middle barrel is missing. It is a shell game, a variant of the guessing-game (with coins in both hands) that Rosencrantz had gently played with Guildenstern at the opening of the act. The lid of the right-hand barrel is raised cautiously, and the heads of Rosencrantz and Guildenstern appear –

present after all. The lid of the left-hand barrel is raised, and the head of the Player – not Hamlet – emerges. Hamlet seems to have vanished in the wrong barrel. The machinery of the plot is here inseparable from the playwright's own joke.

In a more complex and serious fashion, much the same thing happens at the very end of the play. After Guildenstern's attempt to kill the Player and the Player's choreographing of the Tragedians' multiple deaths, the lights fade over the fallen bodies upstage. Downstage, only Guildenstern and Rosencrantz are visible as they make their final comments. And now, in spite of all we have believed about their necessary meeting with death in England, the play shows us no such thing. It is not simply that Stoppard cuts off the action before their arrival and picks it up again at once with the final announcement by the two ambassadors from England 'that Rosencrantz and Guildenstern are dead'. In fact, Rosencrantz and then Guildenstern suddenly disappear from our view in mid-conversation – effectively slain by the light-man's throwing a switch. Death, Guildenstern has earlier said, is 'just a man failing to reappear, that's all – now you see him, now you don't, that's the only thing that's real'. And now, after discovering the absence of his partner ('Rosen –? Guil – ?') he gathers himself to leave: 'Well, we'll know better next time. Now you see me, now you –'. And he disappears. Immediately we cut from that 'death', which is explicitly presented as no less a theatrical illusion than the earlier 'death' of the Player at the hands of Guildenstern, to the court in Denmark. As the lights go up, revealing the 'corpses' of *Hamlet* in the positions last held by the 'dead' Tragedians, the image of absence is again overlaid with a reminder of theatrical presence. After the Ambassadors' announcement, Horatio begins to tell

of deaths put on by cunning and forced cause,
and, in this upshot, purposes mistook
fallen on the inventors' heads . . . .

But this speech fades out with the entire play, overtaken by dark and music.

Rosencrantz and Guildenstern Are Dead has given us not just 'a blinding metaphor about the absurdity of life' or a 'witty commentary' but an active demonstration of the dialectical power inherent in theatrical play, as it variously explores the illusion of absence. It is not surprising that reviewers who missed Stoppard's full intention, and therefore faulted the play for not doing something else, were favourably struck by aspects of Goldby's production that we can now see as thematically quite central. John Russell Taylor, for example, reviewing the London version, thought the 'idea' of the play to be 'simple', but added: 'Derek Goldby's direction is varied in pace and texture, introducing (metaphorically and literally) as much light and shade as possible into the text. Desmond Heeley's Victorian-Jacobean costumes and mouldering Fonthill-gothic sets are stunningly glamorous.' Walter Kerr, reviewing the New York version, thought the play 'one more document in the unreeling existentialist catalogue', marred by its excessive length and by the fact that 'Mr Stoppard himself is watching too closely, is too much with us'. But he was even more appreciative of thematically central aspects of the production. The 'evening's compensations,' he said, 'grow upon one steadily as the stage lights turn from an autumnal gold to a tidal wave of blood-red.' He singled out for special praise the moment when Brian Murray, playing Rosencrantz in this version, 'seems to catch his breath as from an invisible, sickening blow as he realizes that he cannot for the life of him recall when he first heard about death. . . . The written moment, and Mr. Murray's fiercely concentrated realization of it, are brilliant strokes of theater. . . . So is the fidgety scurry of John Wood's slippered feet as Guildenstern tries, with caterpillar tactics, to evade the sound of what his companion is saying, huddling his toes together and clapping his hands over his ears as though his entire body could be blinded if he exerted himself enough.' But that complex moment of writing and acting, of course, exactly renders our seriously playful presence to our own disconcerting absence. Kerr concluded his review by remarking on other elements of the production that in fact carried out an intention he had not detected:

Paul Hecht's chief player is breathtakingly good: a swaggering Villon with a heart turned to ice, he puts all his belief into his own bravura, his upraised hand holding itself firm in the unanswering air, his stance angrily grounded upon an unresponsive earth. Theatrically speaking, everything about Derek Goldby's production is a joy to watch: the preoccupied people from *Hamlet* swirling by in their faintly frosted costumes, the dusty travelling harlequins creeping out of barrels. . . . The evening's pantomime passages – a king retracting himself into sleep, a sweep of grey cloaks over the field of the dead – are beautifully mounted, and Richard Pilbrow's lighting seems to well inside the play and then diminish to the isolated pinpoints on which each of us must stand. The stage is managed as music might be; in time – and despite inevitable reservations – we are overwhelmed by the visual sound.

Kerr's 'reservations' largely dissolve if we recognise that each item in his appreciative catalogue is a skilful theatrical rendering of the main intention of this script, which asks us to collaborate with Stoppard in a knowingly paradoxical engagement with the anxious question: How can 'we' possibly be 'here'? In so playing our feared absence, we richly enact our presence.

4

Logics of the Absurd

In their different ways, *Rosencrantz and Guildenstern Are
Dead* and *Lord Malquist and Mr Moon* embody
Stoppard's recognition that the frequent avant-garde
attempt to absolutise 'absence' and the 'absurd' is quite
fallacious. We can express 'absence' only because we can
overcome that distance, blockage, or objectification. We
can articulate the 'absurd' only because our relative
control over the artistic medium and the world itself
enables us to formulate the paradoxes that finite thought
must always produce. Such plays as Ionesco's *The Chairs*
and Beckett's *Endgame* therefore depend upon what they
seem to deny: our collaborative presence in a coherent if
incompletely explicable world. Ionesco's own career shows
that going 'beyond the absurd' poses no great problem, for
we were never really there in the first place. Recognising
that fact, a playwright can take the 'absurd' more lightly.
And like W. S. Gilbert or Lewis Carroll, he may choose to
isolate and refine for comic purposes some of the 'logics'
through which it can be ordered and communicated.

Logics of the Absurd

That aim, evident throughout Stoppard's career, is especially prominent in two short plays completed soon after the success of *Rosencrantz and Guildenstern Are Dead*. As Stoppard himself said in 'Ambushes for the Audience', *The Real Inspector Hound* and *After Magritte* are attempts 'to bring off a sort of comic coup in pure mechanistic terms'. But they have here a larger interest. In each, an absurd world discloses on inspection as ostensible logic that resolves the absurdity into an intelligible pattern. But because the terms of that resolution are ludicrously hyperbolic, the play seems to suspend itself between 'logic' and 'absurdity', asking us to regard them as mutually sustaining delights. The real logic of such a theatrical event, discernible in its form, resides in the playfulness through which we participate in that paradox.

The notion that performers and patrons are two sides of the same coin, or the same side of two coins, leads straight to *The Real Inspector Hound*, which Stoppard had already begun before his move to London in 1962. After a substantial re-writing, it opened in June 1968, at the Criterion Theatre, where it was directed by Robert Chetwyn. In this one-act farce a parodied murder mystery – complete with a Mrs Drudge who answers the phone by saying, 'Hello, the drawing-room of Lady Muldoon's country residence one morning in early spring?' – arouses and exposes the desires of two hapless members of the audience, sucks them into an improvised repetition of its first two 'acts', and brings about their deaths. Those victims are the theatre critics Moon and Birdboot (played by Richard Briers and Ronnie Barker in the original production), whose fatuous jargon quite predictably seemed to some reviewers of *The Real Inspector Hound* its main point. Once again Stoppard had reason to object.

'The one thing that *The Real Inspector Hound* isn't about
. . . ,' he said in 'Ambushes for the Audience', 'is theatre
critics. I originally conceived a play, exactly the same play,
with simply two members of the audience getting involved
in the play-within-the-play.' As the writing proceeded, it
seemed that theatre critics, a 'known and defined' quantity
easy to 'parody', might stand in for all of us. If the play is
more than a 'comic coup', Stoppard added, 'then it's
about the dangers of wish-fulfillment. But as soon as the
word's out of my mouth I think, shit, it's a play about
these two guys, and they're going along to this play, and
the whole thing is tragic and hilarious and very, very
carefully constructed.' That retort is surely over-stated.
The play's parody of theatre critics, murder mysteries, and
its own procedures is as much a part of its larger subject as
its mocking of the audience. But Stoppard has reluctantly
pointed to the ostensible and hyperbolic logic of the play's
world. Moon and Birdboot try to attain some 'presence' or
'identity' by means of sheer role-playing. But such
attempts, evident in their reviewer's jargon as in their
narcissistic day-dreams of professional or erotic success,
must draw them irresistibly on to a final 'absence' or
death.

Again it is hard to believe that Stoppard was unfamiliar
with Pirandello's 'trilogy of the theatre in the theatre',
which includes (in addition to *Six Characters in Search of
an Author*) two plays that explore the magnetic and
hypnotic attraction of role-playing. *Each in His Own Way*
portrays a performance of a *commedia a chiave* (the
theatrical equivalent of a *roman à clef*) in which members
of the 'audience' find themselves mirrored. Their angry re-
enactment of certain scenes in the 'theatre lobby' leads to
an uproar that stops the play. *Tonight We Improvise*
contains a bickering cast of actors who, when asked to

improvise a Sicilian melodrama, find themselves gradually drawn into an authentic reliving of their assigned parts. In effect if not by conscious design, *The Real Inspector Hound* condenses both motifs and translates them into a freshly parodic form.

Moon, a pretentious second-string critic, is attending this thriller as a substitute for the first-string Higgs, of whose death he obsessively dreams: 'My presence defines his absence, his absence confirms my presence . . . .' The chocolate-munching Birdboot, a critic of plebeian tastes, seeks a less intellectual presence through obsessive amorous intrigues. He has already spent an evening with tonight's ingénue, who plays the role of Felicity, and he intends to make her reputation. But when he sees the leading lady in the role of Lady Cynthia Muldoon, he transfers his erotic and professional attentions to her. The thriller itself has begun with an on-stage corpse that its characters manage to overlook. Its action is punctuated by miraculously well-timed radio announcements of a dangerous madman loose in the foggy swamps around Muldoon Manor, the ringing of a phone that when answered turns out to have a call for no-one among the *dramatis personae*, and the off-stage conversations, day-dreams, and critical pronouncements of Moon and Birdboot. During its second 'act', Inspector Hound arrives on inflated swamp boots, the corpse is discovered, and a mysterious guest named Simon Gascoyne (who, like Birdboot, has suddenly transferred his attentions from Felicity to Cynthia) stumbles on the corpse and is shot by someone in the wings. But if Simon is not the villain after all, who is?

During the ensuing interval, Moon answers the phone, which is now ringing on an empty stage. The call is from Birdboot's anxious wife, but after taking it, he is caught up in a replay of the thriller's first 'act'. With initial embarrassment but increasing enthusiasm, Birdboot finds himself playing the role of Simon – until the moment when he discovers that the on-stage corpse is that of the missing Higgs, whereupon he too is shot by someone in the wings. Returning to the stage in anguish, Moon becomes trapped there when he discovers that Simon and Hound have now occupied the seats of the two critics. As the replay of the thriller proceeds, Moon somewhat uncertainly enters into the role of Inspector Hound: 'I'm going to find out who did this! I want everyone to go to the positions they occupied when the shot was fired –' Indeed, he goes so far as to accuse Birdboot (whom he calls Simon) of having killed the chap he knows to be Higgs (but calls a Canadian named McCoy). But soon Major Magnus, the crippled half-brother of the presumably deceased Lord Albert Muldoon, accuses Moon himself of killing the unknown stranger, cutting the telephone wires, and returning as Inspector Hound. Beginning to doubt his own sanity, Moon admits that he has dreamed of such murder – whereupon, removing his moustaches and leaping out of his wheelchair, Major Magnus declares himself 'the real Inspector Hound,' who has now trapped the criminal. In horror, Moon recognises Magnus–Hound to be Puckeridge, the third-string critic on the same paper, whose envy must have driven him to engineer this plot. When Moon tries to escape, Puckeridge–Magnus–Hound shoots him down, announces that he is also the vanished Albert Muldoon, and embraces Lady Cynthia. Puckeridge may be a madman on the loose, but he has attained within these farcical Pirandellian terms the histrionic 'presence' that the envious Moon and amorous Birdboot had vainly sought.

The play used by Hamlet to convict Claudius of his guilt

(and by Stoppard to half-convict Rosencrantz and Guildenstern of their more ambiguous treachery) was called by Hamlet *The Mousetrap*. It is therefore appropriate that, to convict Moon, Birdboot, himself, and all the rest of us of fashioning our identities out of hackneyed role-playing, Stoppard has here used a parodic version of what was already the longest-running play in London: Agatha Christie's *The Mousetrap*. In Christie's play, five snow-bound guests at Monkswell Manor, a roomy but modest guest house just opened by young Giles and Mollie Ralston, learn from some miraculously well-timed radio announcements that an insane murderer is on the loose. Detective Sergeant Trotter soon arrives on skis (not swamp boots) to inform them that one person in the house must be the murderer and two others must be his next intended victims. As the plot thickens, the telephone line is found to be cut, one guest is murdered, and Trotter himself orders the remaining people to go to the positions that were occupied when the murder occurred. But though he wants them 'to go through these actions a second time,' there's a catch: 'The same actions will be performed,' says Trotter, '*but not necessarily by the same people.*' Having thus arranged to be alone with Mollie, he discloses that he is himself the murderer, engaged in avenging the mistreatment of his brother and sister and himself when they were orphaned as children. Trotter's attempt to kill Mollie is fortunately interrupted by two guests, one of whom, a Major Malcolm, turns out to be a real policeman in disguise. In 'Three Blind Mice'. the story from which Christie adapted the play, Major Malcolm is in fact a real 'Inspector Tanner'.

Stoppard has incorporated wry echoes of many of these details in what seems as much an admiring pastiche as a parody. His own 'repeat performance', of course, goes far beyond Trotter's in giving the same parts to different people, and he has moved the action to an aristocratic country-house with adjacent tennis-court, rather like Lady Tressilian's house in Christie's *Towards Zero*, inhabited by suitably melodramatic characters. He may have drawn some suggestions from A. Conan Doyle's 'The Hound of the Baskervilles', where a baying hound, a foggy countryside, a brother returned from America, a repeated crime, a false Sherlock Holmes, and a disguised corpse are among the data perplexing Holmes and Watson as they try 'to frame some scheme into which all these strange and apparently disconnected episodes could be fitted.' And at least one suggestion seems to have come from Robert Benchley, who remarked, when hearing a phone ring on an empty stage, 'It's for me' – and left the theatre. 'Derivative, of course,' Moon says of the thriller they are watching. 'But quite sound,' adds Birdboot. We may say the same of Stoppard's farce. And we might even echo Moon's turgid answer to his own question about the thriller: 'For what in fact is this play concerned with? It is my belief that here we are concerned with what I have referred to elsewhere as the nature of identity.' The ostensible logic in Moon's and Birdboot's world, ludicrous only because of its hyperbolic and mechanical terms, is that by which our desire for a recognised 'presence' or 'identity' drives us toward inauthenticity, 'absence', and 'death'.

The real logic of this theatrical event, however, is provided by the game of mirrors that enables us to focus and transcend that process. When the stage-lights go up, we see in the upstage gloom 'a bank of plush seats and pale smudges of faces' – in effect, our reflection in a huge mirror. (The device may recall the mirror in Genet's *The Balcony*, which reflects an unmade bed in what should be the first few rows of the orchestra.) Once established, that effect fades out 'until the front row remains to remind us of the rest and then, finally, merely two seats in that row', occupied by our own parodic representatives, Moon and Birdboot. We soon find, of course, that they too are reflected, though unwittingly at first, in the play they are watching; and when they are sucked into it, we observe our own tragicomic fate at a farcical remove. The ingenious correspondences between the first two 'acts' of the thriller and the replay with Birdboot and Moon set up an internal mirroring, which is redoubled and reversed when Moon is trapped on stage and Simon and Hound, occupying the critics' seats, begin to talk like parodies of those already parodic critics. Simpler and more tightly organised than the dialectic of *Rosencrantz and Guildenstern Are Dead,* this game of mirrors invites us to recognise the anxious and inhumane pretensions of our usual ego-life, to relish their absurdity as we slough them off, and to identify ourselves for the duration of the performance with that playful process of liberation.

In Sophocles' *Oedipus Rex* the self-appointed detective finds that he is in fact the criminal. *The Real Inspector Hound* offers a farcical variation on that plot: the 'false' detective, criminal at least in his desires, is shot down by the 'real' detective, who is more successful at the same game. *After Magritte* offers a more charitable version of the same plot: the ingeniously incompetent detective here fails to discover that he is the reality behind the non-existent criminal that he is pursuing. Written soon after the Tate Gallery's retrospective exhibition of René Magritte's paintings in 1969, this farce – which Stoppard called 'not an intellectual play' but 'a nuts-and-bolts-comedy' – was first produced by Ed Berman's Inter-Action Productions at the Ambiance Lunch-Hour Theatre Club (then in the Green Banana Restaurant) in April 1970. Geoffrey Reeves directed and Clive Barker played Inspector Foot. It was the first of several Stoppard plays to be produced by Inter-Action, a group whose off-beat taste, improvisatory techniques, and energetic community involvement he has found attractive.

The opening tableau of *After Magritte* sets before us an apparently surreal image reminiscent of Magritte's painting. In *L'Assassin menacé*, for example, a man is listening intently to a gramophone with an old-fashioned horn, while a naked woman or mannequin, bleeding from the mouth, lies on a nearby sofa, two bowler-hatted detectives stand menacingly on either side of the doorway, and three other figures spy on the scene through a window. Because all have the same face, we suspect a single psychic reality behind that dreamlike configuration. Is the painter inviting us to join him in confessing our multiple roles as murderer, victim, agent of justice, and voyeur? In *After Magritte* we may suspect a similar game. A man in fishing waders is standing on a chair and blowing into a heavy metal lampshade; a shoeless woman in a full-length gown is on her hands and knees staring at the floor; and another woman lies on an ironing board, with a white bath-towel covering her body, a black rubber bathing-cap concealing much of her head and face, and a bowler hat resting on her stomach. Against the door have been piled a settee, chairs, a TV set, a cupboard, and a gramophone with an old-fashioned horn; and through the window we see the shoulders, face, and helmet of a police constable, as motionless as a cut-out figure. Here too, as we begin to search for some hidden reality, we will find it hard to distinguish a criminal from a victim, an agent of justice, or a voyeur.

The action of *After Magritte,* however, complicates and simplifies our search in surprising ways. Police Constable Holmes, after looking through the window, leads Inspector Foot to believe that in this 'disorderly house' (with 'tarted up harpies staggering about drunk' and 'naked men in rubber garments hanging from the lampshade') Reginald and Thelma Harris have 'performed without anaesthetic an illegal operation on a bald nigger minstrel about five-foot-two'. Gradually, however, we will infer rational and commonplace explanations for all of the items in the opening tableau. At the same time, we will learn of another strange appearance, which had led Holmes and Foot to the Harris flat. Shortly after two o'clock that afternoon, as the Harrises' car pulled away from the kerb on Ponsonby Place, where it had received a parking ticket during their visit to the Magritte exhibition at the Tate, Thelma saw on the sidewalk a one-legged footballer with shaving-cream on his face, a football under his arm, and an ivory cane in his hand. Or so she says. Reginald saw a bearded blind man in pyjamas carrying a tortoise. Mother saw a man in prison garb carrying a handbag and a cricket bat. And on the basis of an elderly neighbour's eye-witness account, Inspector Foot is quite certain that the man was a one-legged minstrel carrying a crutch and a stolen cash-box. He therefore proceeds to accuse the Harrises of being accomplices in a robbery that his elaborate inferences persuade him has taken place.

This mystery, too, we solve by a simplifying inference. At the end of the play we hear Foot tell how, while shaving, he himself saw the Harris car pulling away from the kerb outside his residence on Ponsonby Place and then rushed outdoors, both feet jammed in the same pyjama leg, and carrying his wife's handbag and unopened parasol, in hope that he might move his own car before it could receive a parking ticket. But no character in the play, not even Foot, shares our discovery that he was his own imagined criminal. In so confirming our rationality, *After Magritte* sets itself directly against Ionesco's *The Bald Soprano*, in which a series of yet more bizarre coincidences seems to undermine all rationality as it leads to a farcical solution of a mystery. Coming full circle but with an important difference, *After Magritte* ends with a tableau that poses for Holmes a yet more daunting riddle: Mother is standing precariously on one foot, balanced on a chair that is itself on the table, playing her tuba; Reginald, blinded by a cushion-cover and wearing his wife's gown, is also standing on one foot, counting; Thelma is crawling on the floor in her underwear, sniffing; and Foot himself, with one foot bare and his eyes covered by sun-glasses, is eating a banana. Has this alarmingly absurd world now captured even Inspector Foot, who seems to be demanding from Holmes an 'explanation'? Holmes recoils in paralysis. But this time we ourselves have been given in advance a rational explanation for each item in the tableau.

Such a trickily rational procedure seems far from the irrationalism that surrealist art is often said to contain. *After Magritte* differs from Magritte's own work, however, only in the degree to which it asks us to reflect upon its necessary paradoxes. Despite Magritte's refusal to accept any doctrine of 'meaning' or 'explanation' of the world, his painting is surprisingly rational in its exploration of the antinomies that haunt our accounts of perception. And the more farcical logic of *After Magritte* is itself paradoxical. Its characters develop their wild accounts of puzzling appearances by the same process that enables us to reduce those appearances to commonplace events. Though they blind themselves in their haste to find a pattern both rational and imaginative, their weakness seems very much like the power that has generated the world of incisively rational but baroquely imaginative collocations and coincidences in which they must live.

These paradoxes suggest that the play's real logic must be more comprehensive than a Foot could understand even if he were Head of the Yard. In fact, this half-mocking celebration of both rational insight and imaginative blindness is itself governed by an elaborate 'counterweight system' that deploys verbal and visual puns. We are invited to suspect that the meaning of every item in this theatrical event, from the title itself to such words, images, or objects as 'foot', 'tuba', 'language', or 'light', might turn out to be disconcertingly plural. The dramatic movement consists of a repeated disturbing and re-establishing of our mental equilibrium through the addition, modification, and subtraction of such items and their meanings. When one complication disappears, another must take its place to right the balance. When one meaning goes up, another must come down. The counterweight system itself is physically present before us in the light-fixture that Reginald Harris is trying to repair. No longer counter-balanced by the one hundred and fifty lead slugs that Thelma is gathering up from the floor, it requires a basket of fruit, with the subtraction of a bite from an apple or the addition of a hat, to maintain its equilibrium. Similar subsitutions and modifications in the dialogue and action (light-bulbs, a hot-iron, clothing, slugs and a needle, the meanings of words, and states of awareness) comprise the play's forward motion as a continually readjusted system of balances produces both our darkness and our light.

Taking place 'after Magritte' and in the style of Magritte (who is confused by Thelma with Georges Simenon's fictional French detective Maigret) the play is full of playful language. Variations on 'blindness' and 'foot' repeatedly signal the characters' incompetence. But for us the most illuminating bundle of meanings is that conveyed by 'light' itself: as a variously employed electric fixture, a source of visual or mental illumination, or the quality of object or mind that must be counterbalanced by a certain gravity. Proliferating meanings of such kinds weave through the play from beginning to end. The opening gambit, provoked by Reginald Harris's blowing on the hot bulb, uses both deliberate and inadvertent puns:

> THELMA: It's electric, dear.
> HARRIS: (*mildly*) I didn't think it was a flaming torch.
> THELMA: There's no need to use language. That's what I always say.

We have, of course, a need to lighten our lives with language in as many ways as possible. And after this play has helped us to do so for a while, it moves to an appropriate conclusion. The stage is in total darkness as we hear Foot describe his escapade in pyjamas. Just when our final inference illuminates the actual identity of the imagined 'criminal', Mother calls 'Lights!' Coincidentally, Holmes enters and turns on the central fixture, which discloses the playfully self-blinded and one-footed 'balance' of the final tableau. The lampshade of that fixture, however, deprived of the few ounces of counterweight that had been provided by the banana now being eaten by Foot to relieve his migraine, descends inexorably until it touches the tabletop and leaves the stage in darkness.

For two years after completing *After Magritte,* Stoppard put much of his energy into preparing his second major play, *Jumpers*. But in the autumn of 1971, between the final draft of that play and the beginning of rehearsals at the National Theatre, he agreed to provide Ed Berman's participatory theatre company, Dogg's Troupe, with a 'ceremony' for the opening of the Almost Free Theatre. In recent years Stoppard's television commissions (*Teeth* and *Another Moon Called Earth* in 1967, *Neutral Ground* in 1968, and *The Engagement,* an expansion of *The Dissolution of Dominic Boot,* in 1970) had kept him fairly close to the substance of conventional farce or melodrama. The commission from Inter-Action, however, led him to explore another 'logic' of the absurd. Moving on from the informal language-games of *After Magritte,* he engaged yet more closely the view of Ludwig Wittgenstein in *Philosophical Investigations* that every term in a language refers to a bundle of incompletely related but overlapping meanings, and that the effective reference at any moment depends on the 'language-game' we are playing.

The resulting ceremony, *Dogg's Our Pet* (an anagram of Dogg's Troupe, which is itself, as Berman has said, 'an imperfect homonym'), is in some ways much like a standard improvisational exercise in the theatre that is sometimes called 'Gibberish'. In such an exercise, the actors are asked to give a convincing rendering of a scene, either invented at the moment or taken from an existing script, while speaking unintelligible gibberish instead of ordinary language. It is not surprising that Berman's actors contributed much to this very similar ceremony. 'In rehearsal the play profited a great deal from the invention of the Dogg's Troupe,' Stoppard said later, 'and the printed text is as much a description of an event collectively arrived at as an author's script.' Its ostensible logic involves the collision and interaction of two language-games that are absurdly at odds. A workman, who is building a platform from pieces of wood thrown to him by an off-stage helper in response to appropriate monosyllabic commands, soon finds himself surrounded by language in which English words seem to have meanings quite other than those given in a dictionary. That language is first spoken by two school-boys who playfully assist the workman at his task, then by a schoolmaster who counts out small flags to members of the audience and to the other three people on stage, then by a radio sports announcer who lists football results, and finally by a Lady who delivers a gracious dedicatory speech composed of words that in English would be scatological and abusive. Only gradually does the workman realise that his own helper, who has coincidentally given appropriate responses to English commands, must also speak that alien language. Though the script tells us that the workman is 'Charlie', the schoolboys are 'Able' and 'Baker', and the schoolmaster is 'Dogg' – names taken from the military designation of the letters of the alphabet – only the ambiguous 'Dogg' is spoken on stage. And only gradually do we discover that the workman's helper must in fact be named 'Brick'.

The physical action of the play establishes an analogy between the units of language (words and letters) and the units from which Charlie is constructing his platform (planks, slabs, blocks, bricks, and cubes). Different arrangements lead to differently signifying constructions, but players of different games also construe the same constructions differently. Able and Baker use the spare units to build and rebuild a wall on which the letters puzzlingly read DOGG POUT THERE ENDS, and then SHOUT DOGG PERT NEED, and then DONT UPSET DOGG HERE. After the Lady has delivered her speech from the wobbly platform and Charlie has had a final run-in with those who seem to skew or invert his laconic utterances, he mounts the platform to deliver a speech that surprisingly breaks out of his monosyllabic style:

Three points only while I have the platform. Firstly, just because it's been opened, there's no need to run amok kicking footballs through windows and writing on the walls. It's me who's got to keep this place looking new so let's start by leaving it as we find it. Secondly, I can take a joke as well as any man, but I've noticed a lot of language about the place and if there's one thing I can't stand it's language. I forget what the third point is.

That speech, which echoes Thelma's opening remark in *After Magritte* and anticipates Henry Carr's closing remarks in *Travesties,* gives us for the first time in this play an utterance that belongs unambiguously to the English language-game. And at that point Charlie himself rebuilds the wall to read: DOGGS TROUPE THE END.

We can fully understand *Dogg's Our Pet* only in performance, not just because its physical actions are metaphorically significant but also because its real logic is that of pre-linguistic or trans-linguistic play. Though we often share Charlie's bafflement, we catch on fairly soon to the linguistic collision that frustrates and enrages him. Without giving us a bilingual dictionary, Stoppard's ceremony leads us to participate in a nonsense language that makes its own sufficient sense. The most important theatrical communication here is not verbal at all. It occurs through the miming or our ritual game-playing (building with blocks, tossing a ball, counting out flags, trading compliments and insults, making formulaic inquiries and announcements, delivering vacuous speeches), which actors can fill with easily graspable meaning regardless of the precise words they utter. In that respect *Dogg's Our Pet* is admirably designed as participatory theatre for all ages. And its playful logic shows Stoppard again to be, even when most obviously 'verbal', a surprisingly non-verbal playwright.

The immediate sequel to this brief play was a briefer one: *The (15 Minute) Dogg's Troupe Hamlet.* According to Berman, the script for this edited *Hamlet* (a thirteen-minute condensation, followed by a two-minute condensation of the condensation as an encore) was written for the Fun Art Bus in 1972 but was coincidentally misplaced for four years by both Berman and Stoppard. Rediscovered in 1976, it was performed by the Dogg's Troupe on the parapets of the National Theatre as a prelude to *Hamlet* itself. This skit, built on principles already underlying the mimed 'Murder of Gonzago' in *Rosencrantz and Guildenstern Are Dead,* attains the absurd through the sheer vivacity of its hyper-condensation. The free-wheeling logic of Shakespearean allusion, which has powered so much rhetoric in the last few centuries, enables some whimsical pastiche; and the frenetic speed of the recapitulated plot parodies our own mental act of collapsing a poignant tragedy into the nutshell of a cultural phrase-book. In 1979, Stoppard would combine this piece with an improved version of *Dogg's Our Pet* to make the first part of the more substantial *Dogg's Hamlet, Cahoot's Macbeth.* There the playful language of Dogg and the art of Shakespearean allusion would disclose a richness of social and political meaning that is already implicit in the participatory play of these brief *jeux d'esprit*.

5

Ethics and the Moon

Although *Rosencrantz and Guildenstern Are Dead* remains Stoppard's most popular play, *Jumpers* is more brilliant and more substantial. Suppose that we are visiting the Old Vic once again, on an evening in February 1972, when this farcical and troubling vision of the not too distant future was first being presented by the National Theatre under Peter Wood's direction. Before us is a bare stage, with a big screen as backdrop. When the house-lights go down, we hear an off-stage master of ceremonies (played by Graham Crowden, the Player of *Rosencrantz and Guildenstern Are Dead*) introduce at some political victory-party 'the much-missed, much-loved star of the musical stage, the incomparable, magnetic, Dorothy Moore'. A spotlight follows the singer (played by Diana Rigg) toward centre stage. Knowing Stoppard's predilections, we might expect to hear something like an updated version of the 'Twentieth Century Blues' that ends Noel Coward's *Cavalcade*:

> In this strange illusion,
> Chaos and confusion,
> People seem to lose their way.
> What is there to strive for,
> Love or keep alive for? Say –
> Hey, hey, call it a day.

Or perhaps something like the last song in Osborne's *The Entertainer*:

> Why should I care,
> Why should I let it touch me . . . .

But Stoppard's Dotty – unlike Coward's Fanny or Osborne's Archie – cannot even begin her number. When the off-stage musicians give her the opening bars of 'Shine On, Harvest Moon', she forgets the first line, reintroduces herself as the 'unreliable, neurotic Dorothy Moore', falters again, and leaves the stage.

After that fiasco we are taken rapidly through bits of striptease, vaudeville, circus routine, domestic comedy, murder mystery, and television news – all before reaching an extended scene that mainly consists of a quasi-Shavian monologue. In the first bit the stripper, swinging from the chandelier back and forth into the spotlight, finally knocks over a waiter who has wandered into her path. Then eight gymnasts in yellow suits – announced as 'the incredible – RADICAL! – LIBERAL!! – **JUMPERS**!!' – somersault onto the stage. Dotty returns, on the edge of hysteria, and declares them not at all incredible. Then her husband (played by Michael Hordern, the George Riley of *Enter a Free Man*) interrupts in flannels and smoking-jacket to complain of the two-a.m. noise. Dotty turns on him – 'It's my bloody party, George!' – and begins a track-

1. *Rosencrantz and Guildenstern are Dead*, National Theatre Production at the Old Vic Theatre, 1969. Charles Kay as Hamlet.

2. *Rosencrantz and Guildenstern are Dead*, Alvin Theatre, New York, 1967. Brian Murray and John Wood.

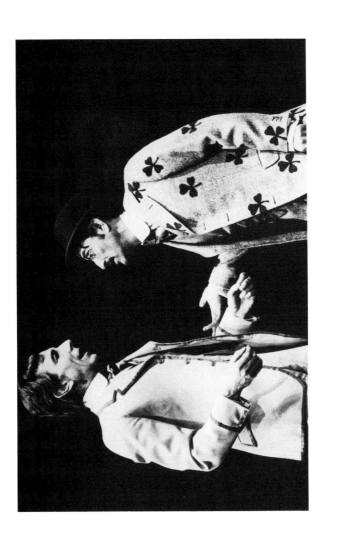

3. *Travesties*, Aldwych Theatre, 1974. John Wood as Henry Carr, Tom Bell as James Joyce.

4. *Jumpers*, Lyttelton Theatre, 1976. National Theatre production with Michael Hordern as George.

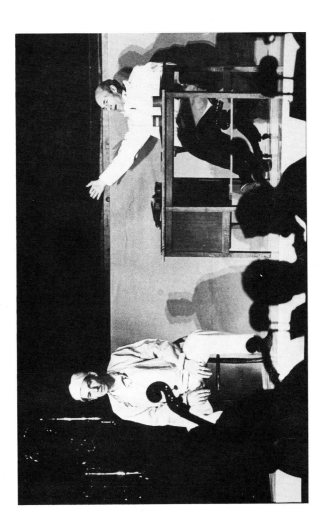

5. *Every Good Boy Deserves Favour*, Royal Shakespeare Company production at the Royal Festival Hall, 1977. Ian McKellen and Patrick Stewart.

6. *'15 Minute' Dogg's Hamlet*, open-air production presented by Inter-Action, 1976.

7. *Night and Day*, ANTA Theatre, New York, 1979. Maggie Smith.

8. *On the Razzle*, Lyttelton Theatre, 1981. Felicity Kendal as Christopher, Ray Brooks as Weinberl.

switching rendition of several moon-songs at once. Downstage the Jumpers assemble themselves into a pyramid, which soon hides her from view. Suddenly there is a shot, which blows one of them out of the pyramid. When Dotty, still the chanteuse, walks through the gap, the dying Jumper pulls himself up against her legs. She holds him, bewildered, as the pyramid collapses. Off-stage a drunk sings, 'It's time to call it a day . . .', and the M.C. announces that the party is over. Dotty calls him – 'Archie . . .' – and he replies: 'Just keep him out of sight till morning. I'll be back'.

Now, as Dotty freezes, the revolving stage wheels the Moores' bedroom, study, and hall into view. The spotlight, focusing on the big screen, becomes first an image of the moon, then a close-up of its surface, and then pictures of rockets and struggling astronauts – a television screen, in fact – as we hear an announcer describe some lunar accident. When the stage-lights finally come up, we see three playing areas. Dotty is in the bedroom holding the corpse; George is in the study working at a pile of manuscripts; and the porter (whom we recognise as last night's waiter) is entering the hall, quietly singing 'Sentimental Journey'. The bedroom TV announces that, after a struggle over who would return to earth on their crippled space capsule, Captain Scott has abandoned Astronaut Oates to his fate on the moon. Dotty flips channels: a military procession, a commercial, and again the moon program – all projected for us on the big screen. We then watch Dotty take off her bloodstained dress, the porter take out a bin of rubbish from what has indeed been a bloody party, and the Secretary (whom we recognise, despite her grim face and trim attire, as last night's stripper) enter the study, put her coat in the wardrobe, and silently prepare to take dictation. Dotty begins quietly to call for help. The bedroom blacks out. Her cries, louder now, echo those of Macduff after Duncan's murder in *Macbeth*: 'Oh, horror, horror, horror! Confusion now hath made its masterpiece . . . !' In the study, trying to ignore what he takes to be his wife's whimsical game, George Moore, professor of moral philosophy, addresses himself to a large mirror in the fourth wall and proceeds to dictate a lecture: 'To begin at the beginning: Is God?'

Trained by film and television to follow such jump-cuts and simultaneities, we recognise that *Jumpers* will engage much more 'Chaos and confusion' than were included in the nostalgic panorama of *Cavalcade*. And we suspect that its questions will be more overwhelming than any posed by Archie in *The Entertainer*. Stoppard's farce is obviously going to explore our twentieth-century witches' brew of technological power, metaphysical uncertainty, neurotic incapacity, and murderous indifference. As a detective story, it has hooked us with the question: Who killed that Jumper? But it soon makes us feel like peripheral characters who have been drawn into a mystery no official investigator can solve. We will ask: Who really cares who killed anybody? Why should *we* care? What grounds have we for our ethical judgements? And what is the shape of the kaleidoscopic performance that draws us into such questions? Looking for answers that elude both the police inspector and the professor of moral philosophy, we will find many of our clues in the idea and the action of 'jumping'.

Who killed that Jumper? If Stoppard has played by the rules that govern detective stories, there are five possibilities: George Moore, the 'tame believer' of his department, who hopes 'to set British philosophy back forty years, which is roughly when it went off the rails'; his wife and former student Dotty, who has retired from the stage because of anxieties apparently induced by man's arrival on the moon; Sir Archibald Jumper, 'doctor of medicine, philosophy, literature and law, with diplomas in psychological medicine and P.T. including gym', who is Vice-Chancellor of the University, leader of the Jumpers, Dotty's close friend and psychiatrist, and master of ceremonies for the victory celebration of the Radical-Liberal Party; Henry Crouch, the porter, who turns out to have been a confidant of the murdered Jumper; and the unnamed Secretary, who never speaks a word but whose body language is enigmatically suggestive. All were in the flat, invisible to us, at the moment when the shot was fired. Aside from the Jumpers and Inspector Bones (who arrives next morning in response to an anonymous telephone call made during the party), they comprise the *dramatis personae*.

We will hear George tell Inspector Bones that he quite disapproves of the Jumpers, a university faculty team of philosopher–gymnasts whose intellectual acrobatics include logical positivism, linguistic analysis, utilitarianism, empiricism, and behaviourism. George himself belongs to 'a school which regards all sudden movements as ill-bred'. He is also a moral intuitionist, like another George Moore, the early twentieth-century author of *Principia Ethica*, whose name he happens most inconveniently to bear. He is therefore quite without academic prestige and would remain so even if he managed to publish his volume of essays – entitled *Language, Truth and God* in apparent defiance of A. J. Ayer's famous *Language, Truth and Logic*, which had encouraged British philosophy to jump the rails in 1936. George is scheduled to deliver his lecture-in-progress on the necessity of belief in God at the annual symposium on 'Man – good, bad or indifferent', to be held this evening. His opponent, he says, will be a professor of logic named Duncan McFee. But as we must infer by late in Act One, McFee is none other than the murdered Jumper. Can envy have tempted our professor of moral philosophy to play Macbeth to this Duncan?

We surely find that notion more incredible than the idea of the Jumpers themselves. A man like McFee could believe that murder is not inherently wrong. With Ayer and many other British philosophers in recent decades, he argued that 'good' and 'bad' are merely conventions that codify our arbitrary if socially useful preferences. But George is averse to such amoral jumping. Kindly, easily embarrassed, tolerant of mistaken views, generous in his remarks about McFee as a person, and respectful of the life of even hares, tortoises, and goldfish, he is passionately devoted to an absolute 'good'. He is also, of course, bumbling and incompetent, habitually abstracted from daily affairs, and quite unable to maintain a satisfactory emotional and sexual intimacy with his troubled wife. His efforts to compose a lecture, which may remind us of Vaclav Havel's *The Difficulty of Concentration*, contain much mental jumping – the self-revising tics of an anxious academic mind. And his domestic problems are essentially those of Stoppard's Mr Moon. Moreover, George clearly knows nothing of McFee's death until late in Act Two. Assuming that his own anonymous complaint about the noise has brought Inspector Bones to the flat, he completely misses the inspector's reference to 'a professor picked off while doing handsprings for a cabaret'. Dotty finds it all too easy (thanks in part to a trick cupboard door borrowed from Robert Dhery's *La Plume de ma Tante*) to hide McFee's body from George whenever he enters the bedroom. Some farcical misunderstandings lead both Bones and Dotty to think that George wants to accept responsibility for the murder (and lead George to think that Dotty has killed and eaten his pet hare, Thumper), but George himself is stunned when Sir Archibald Jumper tells him, late in Act Two, that McFee 'shot himself this morning, in the park, in a plastic bag'. And he is doubly stunned a few minutes later when Crouch reveals that he too had phoned the police and that he thinks Dotty has murdered McFee.

Despite George's good intentions, however, we cannot declare him completely innocent. Not only has he been unable and perhaps unwilling to help Dotty in her psychological difficulties; he is also capable of an unwitting violence that is for him, at least, tantamount to murder. In fact, he *has* shot a 'jumper'. In the closing moments of Act Two, we discover with George that earlier in the day, as he was rehearsing with bow and arrow a demonstration of one of Zeno's paradoxes, the arrow he let fly (because Dotty called out 'Fire!' from the bedroom) had hit his pet hare, who had previously jumped on top of the wardrobe. In his grief and remorse over that discovery, George accidentally steps down from the chair on which he is standing – right onto his pet tortoise, Pat. This second inadvertent killing almost seems an act of self-destruction, for if Thumper is a jumper, Pat is rather more like George himself. Aesop's fable of the hare and the tortoise, which George has already confused with Zeno's paradox of Achilles and the tortoise, now suggests to us a farcical race in which both parties lose. Holding Thumper aloft impaled on the arrow as he stands with one foot on the chair and the other on the crushed Pat, George cries, 'Dotty! Help! Murder!' That self-implicating cry echoes and reverses Dotty's own cries from the bedroom at the beginning of Act One, which he had failed to take seriously.

91

Did Dotty kill McFee? Bones thinks so, though he urges that this 'highly strung' and 'delicate' singer whom he idolises be helped to escape the law's full force by means of a plea of insanity. Archie Jumper may also think so, though he may not be defending *her* when he has the corpse removed in a plastic bag, certifies as coroner that McFee committed suicide, tries to bribe Bones with cash or a better job, and finally traps him – with Dotty's apparent help – in what can be made to look like attempted rape. If Dotty's distraught state of mind impelled her to shoot McFee, she might be as ambiguously guilty-and-innocent of his death as George is of Thumper's and Pat's. Her manner does suggest an imperfectly repressed violence against herself and others. Like Jane Moon in *Lord Malquist and Mr Moon,* she is a hysterical exhibitionist who flaunts her sexuality while withholding herself from her husband and perhaps from everyone. (Though she seems to grant special favors to Archie, we do not know what goes on in that four-poster bed. Perhaps, as he says, merely a dermatographic examination.) When she effectively traps the admiring Bones by crying 'Rape!' she may not have been trying to escape from the law. Archie himself had dismissed her earlier cry of 'Murder!' as 'just exhibitionism: what we psychiatrists call "a cry for help"'. And to Bones' objection – 'But it *was* cry for help' – he had replied with psychiatric circularity: "*All* exhibitionism is a cry for help, but a cry for help *as such* is only exhibitionism'. We do know, of course, that her cries all morning have been embroidering upon her dismay over McFee's death.

We discover, too, that this apparently frivolous and game-playing woman has been shocked into her present state by the ethical implications of the moon-landings. Like Penelope in *Another Moon Called Earth*, she has been deeply disturbed by their apparent exposure of the ultimate groundlessness of all our ethical postulates. By late in Act Two we are fairly certain that her bitter frivolity is born of despair. Though mocking George's search for a philosophical absolute and taking delight in Archie's amoral pragmatism, she can break out – or break down – into a moving prophetic diatribe:

Well, it's all over now. Not only are we no longer the still centre of God's universe, we're not even uniquely graced by his footprints in man's image. . . . Man is on the Moon, his feet on solid ground, and he has seen us whole, all in one go, *little – local* . . . and all our absolutes, the thou-shalts and the thou-shalt nots that seemed to be the very condition of our existence, how did *they* look to the two moonmen with a single neck to save between them? Like the local customs of another place. When that thought drips through to the bottom, people won't just carry on. There is going to be such . . . breakage, such gnashing of unclean meats, such covetting of neighbours' oxen and knowing of neighbours' wives, such dishonourings of mothers and fathers, and bowings and scrapings to images graven and incarnate, such killing of goldfish and maybe more – [*Looks up, tear-stained*] Because the truths that have been taken on trust, they've never had edges before, there was no vantage point to stand on and see where they stopped.

She weeps, and Archie responds with a psychiatric reduction that merely confirms her vision of our loss of ethical categories: 'When did you first become aware of these feelings?' She turns to George, but he will not or cannot respond at all.

Our sympathies here are with Dotty, whatever the naïveté of her despairing relativism and whatever her moral or legal guilt. We know that she has actually killed the Moores' goldfish – much to the indignation of George, who calls it 'murder' – in order to play a symptomatic charade about 'The Moon and Sixpence'. We cannot deny that prophetic outrage might have impelled a mentally disturbed woman to shoot a Jumper who seems to exemplify the evaporation of absolutes. But when George returns to the bedroom a few minutes later, stunned by Crouch's disclosures, we are prepared to believe her rather casual response:

> GEORGE: Crouch says McFee was shot! – here – last night – He thinks Dorothy did it –
> DOROTHY: I thought Archie did it. *You* didn't do it, did you Georgie? [*Disappears into Bathroom*]

Archie insists that they just do not know who did it, but George, picking up a motif from his lecture-in-progress, declares: 'There are many things I know which are not verifiable but nobody can tell me I don't know them, and I think that I know that something happened to poor Dotty and she somehow killed McFee, as sure as she killed my poor Thumper'. A few minutes later, of course, George learns that *he* killed Thumper. Partly because of his evident mistake, we are inclined by the end of Act Two to risk this modest leap of faith: we think that we know, or at least we hope, that neither George nor Dotty killed McFee.

Did Archie do it? Sir Archibald Jumper is in effect a Lord Malquist who has acquired the intellectual and political arts of a pragmatic and pseudo-democratic society. He is the stylist as man of power, the engagingly aristocratic villain as embodiment of all that is most duplicitous in our anti-aristocratic time. His initials may remind us of A. J. Ayer, the Oxford philosopher whose logical dissolving of metaphysical and ethical propositions seems to permit his manoeuvres. His philandering psychiatry may remind us of Joe Orton's *What the Butler Saw*, where psychiatry itself becomes an image of our insane manipulation of each other. Archie is also for us the Radical-Liberal Party, which masks its will to power with a rhetoric of liberation and a shrewd observance of social decorum. It is clear from his behaviour and from Dotty's reports that he will use any means to advance his own ends. Every move he makes in apparent defence of her may really be in self-defence – even when he disarmingly suggests to Bones that 'anybody could have fired the shot, and anybody could have had a reason for doing so, including, incidentally, myself'. Bones pricks up his ears and respectfully asks for a motive. The reply seems implausible: 'Who knows? Perhaps McFee, my faithful protégé, had secretly turned against me, gone off the rails and decided that he was St Paul to Moore's Messiah'. When Bones questions the importance of such a jump backward, Archie replies that if McFee, the 'guardian and figurehead of philosophical orthodoxy', had ever 'threatened to start calling on his masters to return to the true path, then I'm afraid it would certainly have been an ice-pick in the back of the skull'. At this point Dotty calls – 'Darling!' – and Archie modulates out of his sinister fancy: 'And then again, perhaps it was Dorothy. Or someone'. And he smiles.

Bones does not take this hypothetical self-incrimination very seriously, and we ourselves put little credence in such an arch account of a possible rebellion in the ranks. But by the end of Act Two, when Crouch innocently tells Archie a good deal about his friend and mentor McFee, we learn that the professor of logic had indeed gone through a crisis of belief in response to just such events as have affected Dotty: 'It was the astronauts fighting on the Moon that finally turned him, sir'. McFee had come to believe that he was 'giving philosophical respectability to a new pragmatism in public life, of which there have been many disturbing examples both here and on the moon'. He kept recalling that the first Oates, a member of the Antarctic expedition led by the first Scott, had sacrificed his life 'to give his companions a slim chance of survival'. If such altruism is a possibility, he had said to Crouch, 'my argument is up a gum-tree'. Crouch had assured McFee that the more recent Captain Scott, who abandoned Astronaut Oates on the moon, 'is good for twenty years hard'; but McFee had retorted: 'yes *maybe*, but when he comes out, he's going to find he was only twenty years ahead of his time. I have seen the future, Henry, . . . and it's yellow'. When Crouch discloses that the disillusioned McFee had decided to enter a monastery, Archie's disarming hypothesis suddenly seems to us a major clue.

This suspicion, however, must compete with another that has also arisen as we were listening to Archie's conversation with Crouch in the hall. We had never seriously imagined that Crouch might be the murderer. His report to George of his phone call to the police had the ring of truth, and his explanation to Archie of his chats with McFee while the professor was waiting for his girlfriend has now placed him above any reasonable suspicion. Nor had we seriously suspected the Secretary, though we may have noticed a signal pass between her and Archie at the end of Act One, when he arrived with the Jumpers to dispose of the body. But as Crouch said that McFee's girl was none other than the Secretary, we saw her come forward in the study, 'grim, tense, unsmiling', to look at herself in the fourth-wall mirror before getting her coat from the wardrobe. Then, as he told how McFee had broken with her to enter a monastery, her action seemed to underline a possible consequence: 'And now he's dead,' said Crouch, and the Secretary snapped shut her handbag. A clue from the playwright himself? Did *she* kill McFee?

Archie sums up the mystery by saying: 'The truth to us philosophers, Mr Crouch, is always an interim judgement. We will never even know for certain who did shoot McFee. Unlike mystery novels, life does not guarantee a dénouement; and if it came, how would one know whether to believe it?' If Archie is right, *Jumpers* is an agnostic sequel to the ironic plots of *The Real Inspector Hound* and *After Magritte.* But his agnosticism may be the mask of a murderer. And immediately after his bland assertion, we momentarily glimpse a dénouement. The Secretary, turning to leave the study, discloses on the back of her white coat a splash of blood. Of course, George discovers at once that the blood is Thumper's, which has dripped down into the wardrobe. But we may suddenly recall that just before the killing of McFee we had seen her knock down Crouch. In any case, a symbolic connection seems to have been made. Though we may never know who shot McFee, we have two prime suspects, who may have been in league with each other.

Does the Coda, which presents in bizarre dream-form the symposium on 'Man – good, bad or indifferent', help us to settle the question? George is here absurdly ineffective in his appeal to 'the testimony of such witnesses as Zeno Evil, St Thomas Augustine, Jesus Moore and my late friend the late Herr Thumper who was as innocent as a rainbow', while Archie not only wins the debate but also executes a political powerplay that seems to repeat the murder of a renegade Jumper. Samuel Clegthorpe, the former veterinarian and Radical-Liberal spokesman for agriculture who has become Archbishop of Canterbury, is now turning against government policy. As pastor of a human flock, he feels some sympathy for man's irrational beliefs. Archie denounces those sentiments: 'Archbishop, the cat has already jumped'. And Archie's next two speeches portray him as a British ruler quite prepared to liquidate his clerical opponent. 'My Lord Archbishop,' he says, as if he were Shakespeare's Richard III addressing the Bishop of Ely whom he will soon condemn to death, 'when I was last in Lambeth I saw good strawberries in your garden – I do beseech you send for some.' When Clegthorpe starts to explain his shift of position, Archie then echoes Henry II urging the murder of Thomas à Becket: *'Will no one rid me of this turbulent priest?'* Swiftly the Jumpers incorporate Clegthorpe into a pyramid; there is a gunshot; and Clegthorpe is dead. Archie soon caps George's peroration with an ironic wisdom borrowed from Samuel Beckett: 'Do not despair – many are happy much of the time; more eat than starve, more are healthy than sick, more curable than dying; not so many dying as dead; and one of the thieves was saved'. And he even expresses Stoppard's own acknowledgment of that indebtedness by giving to Vladimir's poignant speech in *Waiting for Godot* ('Astride of a grave and a difficult birth. Down in the hole, lingeringly, the grave-digger puts on the forceps . . . .') an astonishingly jazzy transformation: 'At the graveside the undertaker doffs his top hat and impregnates the prettiest mourner. Wham, bam, thank you Sam'. But the Coda has unmistakably cast him as an instigator of murder.

Can we believe it? This Coda is for George what the Circe episode in Joyce's *Ulysses* is for Leopold Bloom: an expressionistic rendering of a subjective state. After

crushing the tortoise and crying out for Dorothy, George
had fallen to the floor, and his amplified sobs had led from
the end of Act Two directly into the symposium. He knows
nothing of the Secretary's possible motives. This is *his*
solution to the mystery, which Stoppard has complicated
by making Archie into an ironic *raisonneur*. The Coda
therefore enables us to decide no matters of fact.
Nevertheless, like the play as a whole, it invites us to share
an unambiguous urgency in matters of conscience. But
here is another set of difficulties. *Jumpers* has baffled and
entertained us with a range of violence, and a range of
possible guilt, in order to make clear that its most
important mysteries are not factual at all but ethical.

Who really cares who killed anybody? And why? For
Bones the death of McFee is no more than a case, and
justice itself is a hobby. He is a farcical image of our own
most superficial response to this play: 'Show business is
my main interest,' he says, 'closely followed by crime
detection.' Even his concern for Dotty's welfare results
from his susceptibility to her theatrical glamour. For Sir
Archibald Jumper the death of McFee is a more serious
business. He wants to eliminate it from the record, and his
method is that of the Radical-Liberal party: 'No problem
is insoluble given a big enough plastic bag'. He is a
chillingly comic image of our pragmatic worlds of
business, politics, and professionalism. For Crouch and
the Secretary, no doubt, McFee's death is a more personal
affair. The porter has experienced the loss of a kindly
professor who had taught him the chess-games of modern
logic: 'a terrible thing, his death'. The Secretary has
endured and may even have produced an ironic sequel to
her recent abandonment. Both outrage and satisfaction
may hide behind her grim mask. But would those two

minor characters care at all if death had not so closely touched their own lives?

Dotty's caring is a more wildly extravagant anguish, masked by irony, a response to a future in which all human beings may become mere objects to be used or eliminated. And yet she seems to have turned herself into an elusive sexual object in order to manipulate such frustrated or powerful objects as George, Bones, and Archie. George's caring is no less inclusive and no less questionable. His ethical obsessions repeatedly tempt him away from the actual world, leading him (as his dreamwork punningly puts it) to 'Zeno Evil'. While composing arguments for belief in God, he ignores his wife's hysteria and misses the fact of murder in the next room. Grieving over the death of a hare, he kills a tortoise. In fact, both Dotty and George allow a universal concern to distract them from more immediate personal and domestic problems about which they might conceivably do something. That is why such ethically serious characters can become figures of farce. One indentifiable 'evil' in *Jumpers* is our all-too-human readiness to escape into passionate talk about ethics and the moon instead of answering our neighbour's cry of pain.

Jumpers can lead us to that reflection, however, only because it assumes that we share Dotty's and George's sensitivities but not their incapacities – and that we will therefore regard the murder of McFee or anyone else with an ethical concern that is more rational and more perceptive than that exhibited by any character in the play. As we watch *Jumpers*, that assumption seems correct but also unjustifiable – for why should we care? The Jumpers' 'main-stream' philosophy reduces our ethical judgements to arbitrary feelings. George's philosophising leads to what he himself calls a 'mysticism of staggering banality'. In fact, Stoppard has ambushed us. If we think of ourselves as fairly sophisticated, more or less agnostic, and yet ethically sensitive human beings, we discover that we are in a philosophical bind. It is amusing to see how the play has caught even A. J. Ayer in that bind. In *Language, Truth and Logic,* he had argued that a word like 'right' or 'wrong' serves merely as an exclamation point, indicating that 'it is attended by certain feelings in the speaker'. But when he reviewed *Jumpers* for the *Sunday Times* (under the title of 'Love Among the Logical Positivists'), that doctrine of 'emotivism' was not in evidence. 'What finally happens to the hare and the tortoise is the most moving moment of the play,' he said, quite as if his own feelings were normative or the ethical substance of the play were objective fact. Of course, Ayer predictably insisted that we require no 'religious sanction' for humane feelings, and that George's muddled attempts are therefore needless. 'Even logical positivists,' he said, 'are capable of love.' But that disarming statement begs the question. Stoppard has shaped a world in which the loss of belief in normative values has unleashed an inhumane will to power. No doubt Archie Jumper would agree that he is capable of love – but why should he bother with that inconvenient feeling? If there is no universal structure of values, humane feelings are no better than any others. Why should anyone believe that love is a 'good' and murder an 'evil'? *Jumpers* makes us demand an answer to that question.

In other words, our concern over the deaths of a Jumper, a hare, a goldfish, and a tortoise has led to a concern over the so-called death of God. At one point Dotty teases George about his apparent belief that 'the non-existent God who is presumed dead' might be 'only missing in action, shot down behind the thin yellow lines of the advancing Rad-Libs and getting himself together to go

101

BOO!' Having failed to prove the existence of that God, George dreams that Archie taunts him in the symposium with a parody of Voltaire's remark that if God did not exist He would have to be invented: 'If the necessary being isn't, surely mother of invention as Voltaire said . . . .' *Jumpers* does not claim, however, that we must invent a cogent doctrine of God this very minute in order to begin living humane lives. Nor is it simply a debate between agnosticism and theism. As Stoppard once wrote to Kenneth Tynan, 'it is a mistake to assume that plays are the end-products of ideas (which would be limiting): the ideas are the end-products of the plays'. And this play suggests that we already share an intuitive, if philosophically unjustified, ethic. We know, for example, that Duncan McFee proceeded from an intuitive judgement of courageous altruism toward a leap of faith in God. But we also know the ironic ethical consequences of his ensuing action: having condemned Scott for abandoning Oates on the moon, he then abandoned his own girl for a monastery. *Jumpers* repeatedly asks us, in fact, to experience the interplay of three modes of interpreting life: an agnostic empiricism that serves the will to power; an anxious religious demand or faith that can be practically and ethically blind; and a spontaneous and compassionate ethical response that helps to guide us through the play's action. Each mode has its own kind of jumping – amoral, anxious, or theatrical – which contributes to the kaleidoscopic whirl of performance.

Some critics, of course, have found that performance undramatic. Reviewing the New York production of 1974 (also directed by Peter Wood, but with shifting jack-knife sets by Josef Svoboda), Martin Gottfried said that 'as stagecraft *Jumpers* isn't', and Harold Clurman complained: 'Its point or "thesis" is not revealed through action: it is only stated. There is no basic confrontation, conflict, or delineation of real characters'. But such comments reveal a surprising inability to grasp the procedures of a stylised but poignant farce that asks us to participate in its own high-spirited jumping. Clive Barnes more accurately noted that the 'framework to the humor is the disarticulated sense of situation comedy that owes so much to radio and television'. Jack Kroll rightly praised 'an astonishing and immensely appealing theatrical form' that, parodying several genres, adds up to 'a metaphysical farce'. And Kenneth Tynan later quoted with approval Geoffrey Reeves' apt remark that *Jumpers* 'uses the stage *as* a stage, not as an extension of TV or the novel'.

Using the stage *as* a stage, *Jumpers* invites us to relish with both sympathy and intellectual detachment what are not 'real characters' so much as brilliant roles, which the actors can fill with their own histrionic life. Through a Graham Crowden (or, in the New York production, a Remak Ramsey) we can explore Archie's self-consciously amoral jumping: his suave refusal to be bound by any previous assumptions or commitments. Through a Diana Rigg and a Michael Hordern (or, in New York, a Jill Clayburgh and a Brian Bedford) we can explore the Moores' neurotic jumping: her track-switching moon songs and evasive charades, his perpetually revised lecture, their absurdly zigzag conversations. (Hordern, said Kenneth Tynan, 'had the part of his life: quivering with affronted dignity, patrolling the stage like a neurotic sentry, his face infested with tics, his fists plunging furiously into his cardigan pockets, he was matchlessly silly and serious at the same time'.) We see that Archie's competence rests on a negation of ethics, and that the Moores' helplessness arises from an anxiety about ethical questions that has become self-obfuscating. But we also see that our own theatrical jumping supplies what is missing. For, moment by moment, the contrapuntal texture of the performance – which includes TV channel-flipping, absurd puns and non-sequiturs, spliced dialogues, synchronised actions, coincidental sound effects, and a hash of parodied genres – leads our sympathetic but detached attention into an ever-widening field of signs that the time is out of joint.

After the cuts and simultaneities of its opening moments, the play continues to engage us in just such theatrical jumping. We repeatedly attend to two or more characters, often in different playing areas, who do not grasp each other's situation. Our amusement and sympathy depend on our ability to jump from one to another, reading the larger pattern of events more accurately than any character can do. Act One proceeds immediately with a counterpoint between the anguished Dotty and the oblivious George. His lecture-in-progress is punctuated by cries from the blacked-out bedroom, often with a comic effect that she cannot and he will not appreciate. Their ensuing conversation in the bedroom, broken up by their own distracted jumps, requires our understanding of their misunderstandings, our recognition of the emotional distance that frustrates their moments of potential intimacy, and our ability to see that even when George 'correctly' reads such charades as *The Naked and the Dead* and *The Moon and Sixpence* he has not grasped their meaning as hysterical cries for help. When he returns to the study, the lights remain on in the bedroom, allowing us to watch Dotty place McFee's body in a chair as George resumes his lecture. We are therefore prepared to appreciate from both points of view the effect of his sudden re-entry into the bedroom. Dotty's impromptu and defensive charade – in which she disrobes in order to mask the body – is read by George as 'Lulu's back in town', but for us it is a variation on *The Naked and the Dead*.

When Bones arrives, such counterpoint becomes more complex. George's ignorance of the crime now collides with Bones's ignorance of his ignorance – and soon with Dotty's, too. *Jumpers* also begins now to engage in a self-parody that further emphasises our awareness of meanings inaccessible to the characters. George, who has been intermittently preparing to shave, meets Bones at the door with his face covered with lather and a tortoise in his hand – a retake of the enigmatic image that caused Inspector Foot so much trouble in *After Magritte*. Dotty's 'romantic' meeting with Bones in the bedroom is farcically amplified by a coincidental sound-track that emanates, as we soon discover, from the study, where it forms part of George's absurdly earnest lecture. And finally, in a scene that asks us to observe actions in the study, hall, and bedroom, the Secretary types while Dotty mimes 'Sentimental Journey' to the accompaniment of her own recorded singing, and Archie engineers a removal of the body by Jumpers whose movements are choreographed to fit the music. Like Dotty's charades, this riddling collocation of disparate elements is a sign that we must try to interpret as we grope toward a larger pattern of meaning.

Act Two repeats and complicates such movements as Bones now presses his attack, Archie engages in various defensive manoeuvres, and Dotty's ambiguous relation to Archie becomes for us an important secondary question. The Act begins, for example, with a farcical conversation between Bones and George in the hall, which is accompanied by Dotty's recorded song 'Forget Yesterday' (with its Coward-like motif: 'Call it a day but wait for the night') emanating from the blacked-out bedroom where she and Archie are now alone together. Archie's examination of Dotty with the 'dermatograph' will also give us another image of our interpretive jumping: 'All kinds of disturbances under the skin', he says, 'show up on the surface, if we can learn to read it, and we are learning.' As Archie traps Bones, George belatedly discovers the murder, and we refine our understanding of the play's ethical, psychological, and philosophical issues, we are 'learning to read' Stoppard's enigmatic surfaces with a combination of skill and humane concern that neither its anxious nor its amoral jumpers permit themselves.

Jumpers makes thematic use of the traditional tension in farce between a vision of great disorder and a style of heightened and accelerated order. The action on stage suggests an apocalyptic disarray, as technological power overwhelms ethical wisdom. But we understand that action by sharing in the play's ethically informed jumping from image to image. Finally, *Jumpers* becomes a kind of anti-farcical farce, almost a high comedy, for, like Shakespeare's *Twelve Night* or Molière's *The Misanthrope*, it leads us to see the need for that intelligent sympathy which farce always invites us to suppress. Its expressionistic Coda sums up these points by translating our theatrical jumping into a boldly accelerated, allusive, and self-parodying style that fuses the objective and the subjective. Setting George's tribute to 'the late Herr Thumper who was as innocent as a rainbow' against Archie's 'Wham, bam, thank you Sam', it gives us a doubly self-ironic recapitulation of the play's serious commitment to both ethics and art. Rather like Chekhovian comedy, *Jumpers* has asked us to find in ourselves, as we share in its contrapuntal form, an enacted response to questions that must here remain without explicit answer. Mr Moon, in Stoppard's novel, had decided that madness is 'the ultimate rationalisation of the private view'. *Jumpers* allows us to understand and surmount such madness by means of a sane and implicitly ethical wholeness of apperception. It therefore embodies what Stoppard has considered the most important quality of serious art. In 'Ambushes for the Audience' he said: 'Briefly, art – Auden or Fugard or the entire cauldron – is important because it provides the moral matrix, the moral sensibility, from which we make our judgements of the world'. In such later pieces as *Every Good Boy Deserves Favour*, *Professional Foul*, and *Night and Day*, Stoppard's political judgements would become yet more explicit. But *Jumpers* remains his richest and most compelling exploration of the ethical issues we must face as we act in a human world.

6

The Prism of Travesty

Jumpers invites of us, as actors and witnesses, an attentive ethical concern that we can observe nowhere within the ominously absurd world we are playing. *Travesties* proposes a yet trickier game. It asks us to refract both the content and the style of our playing through an ironic prism that illuminates several large questions: How do we make art? Or revolution? Or history? Or, indeed, any kind of meaning?

Suppose we are at the Aldwych Theatre on a June evening in 1974, when *Travesties* was first being performed by the Royal Shakespeare Company under Peter Wood's direction. The lights come up on what seems a section of the Zurich Public Library, though at downstage right we also see a dimly lit piano and an old man (played by John Wood) whom we infer to be Henry Carr. At the library tables, busy with their books and papers, are Tristan Tzara (played by John Hurt), James Joyce (Tom Bell), and Lenin (Frank Windsor). With Joyce is a young woman (Maria Aitken) who must be Gwendolen. During the next few minutes we watch a bizarre series of disturbances in the library.

Tzara first reads out (in a Rumanian accent) an English poem that he has just composed, according to his Dada recipe, by cutting up what he has written and shaking the words out of a hat. If we pay close attention to its incoherent lines, we may discover that we are hearing intelligible French. 'Ill raced alas whispers kill later nut east', for example, sounds rather like 'Il reste à la Suisse parce qu'il est un artiste'. But who has made coherent meaning from those fragments – Tzara, Stoppard, or we ourselves? ('Sssssssh!' says the librarian Cecily, played by Beth Morris, as she enters and crosses the stage.) Joyce then dictates to Gwendolen some obscure invocations: 'Deshill holles eamus', 'Send us bright one, light one, Horhorn, quickening and wombfruit', and 'Hoopsa, boyaboy, hoopsa!' If we have read *Ulysses*, we may recognise bits from the Oxen of the Sun episode, which, as it recounts the birth of a baby, recapitulates in pastiche and parody the history of English prose. ('Sssssssh!' says Cecily again.) After an accidental swapping of two folders, which leaves Cecily with Joyce's manuscript when she thinks she has Lenin's, and Gwendolen with Lenin's when she thinks she has Joyce's, Lenin begins to speak in Russian with his wife Nadya (Barbara Leigh-Hunt), who has just entered. If we understand that language, we know that Nadya is reporting a revolution in St Petersburg and a rumour of the Tzar's imminent abdication. Meanwhile Joyce is now walking about, searching in his pockets for scraps of paper that contain phrases he may want to use in *Ulysses*, and reading them out. Retrieving another scrap from the floor, he reads: 'GEC (USA) 250 million marks, 28,000 workers . . . profit 254,000,000 marks'. But that scrap has been dropped by Lenin, who now engages

Joyce with quadrilingual courtesy: 'Pardon! . . . Entschuldigung! . . . Scusi! . . . Excuse me!' Finally Joyce exits, declaiming a limerick about a 'librarianness of Zurisssh' (which Cecily, entering, fortuitously completes with another 'Sssssssh!') and singing 'Galway Bay' – a tune that Carr now picks up on the piano as the set changes from the Library to his room. As he begins to speak, we realise that this scrappy and imperfectly intelligible counterpoint of languages, arts, and revolutions has been a Prologue to the old man's retrospective meditation, itself a thing of shreds and patches. And we will soon find that it also serves as a Joycean overture to a play that repeatedly asks us to collaborate in transforming other people's fragments into fresh meaning.

As the main character on his own historical stage, 'Carr of the Consulate' begins by recalling how he had known Joyce when he was writing *Ulysses*, had shaken Lenin's hand before he was known to the world as Lenin, had lived through the early days of Dada, and had even taken part in a play produced by Joyce, achieving a 'personal triumph in the demanding role of Ernest, not Ernest, the other one, in at the top, have we got the cucumber sandwiches for Lady Bracknell' – all in that Switzerland of 1917 which was for artists and other refugees 'the still centre of the wheel of war'. Though Carr's bits of narrative and semi-soliloquy seem a travesty of both 'history' and 'art', we may doubt (after the Prologue) that greater minds have been much less egocentric and scrappy. Nevertheless, because the Prologue had also prepared us for something more sharply ironic than Carr's self-indulgent aestheticism seems likely to provide, we expect some parodic variations on his account. We do not have to wait long. His fatuous rhetoric has already absurdly applied the same formulas to Joyce, Lenin, and Dada. And when, removing hat and dressing-gown and letting the crustiness of age disappear from his voice, John Wood suddenly becomes the young Carr of 1917, we find that yet bolder patterns of repetition give ironic shape to the ensuing flashbacks.

A manservant enters with a tray of tea things and sandwiches, almost as if he were Lane in Wilde's *The Importance of Being Earnest.* It is Bennett, played by John Bott. With more than a little help from Stoppard, Carr is already imagining his early life as something out of that 'theatrical event of the first water' in which he had played not Ernest but 'the other one', Algernon Moncrieff. He has cast himself as a British Consul rather like the aesthete Algernon, with a sartorial obsession that will assume for us a thematic importance. More than once this play will remind us of Carlyle's *Sartor Resartus* (or 'the tailor retailored'), in which history is reconstituted from scraps of paper and a 'clothes philosophy' explains the changing world of appearance. As Carr now re-imagines what led up to his meetings with Tzara, Joyce, and Lenin, he goes through five variations on Algy's opening conversation with Lane, each introduced by a 'time-slip' and Bennett's repeated line: 'I have put the newspapers and telegrams on the sideboard, sir'. But who *was* this 'manservant' Bennett? At the end of the play old Cecily will make old Carr confess that Bennett, and not Carr, had been the British Consul in Zurich.

When Bennett-Lane announces Tzara, the pastiche of Wilde's play continues without a hitch: 'How are you, my dear Tristan?' says Carr-Algy. 'What brings you here?' And quite as if he were John (alias Ernest) Worthing transformed into a Rumanian nonsense, Tzara answers: 'Plaizure, plaizure! What else? Eating ez usual, I see 'Enri?!' The arrival of Tzara here leads directly to that of Gwendolen (Carr's sister, cast in his memory as Wilde's

111

Gwendolen) and Joyce (an Irish nonsense, cast as Lady Bracknell), and then into a manic explosion of shared limericks. But the scene between Carr-Algy and Tzara-Jack will be twice repeated at greater length as *Travesties* edges toward a fuller engagement with Wilde's script and with its own themes of art, revolution, and history.

'I don't know how radical you are,' Lenin once said to a Rumanian Dadaist in Zurich, 'or how radical I am. I am certainly not radical enough; that is, one must be always as radical as reality itself.' But how radical would that be? What is the 'reality' to which our so-called 'radicals' are always inadequate? *Travesties* plays with that question through its dialectic of flashbacks. Stoppard had prepared for this use of flashbacks in two recent pieces for radio. *Where Are They Now* (1970) cuts back and forth between 1969 and 1947 as it probes the lives of some Old Boys from a public school. The more elaborate *Artist Descending a Staircase* (1972), which Stoppard has called a 'dry run' for *Travesties*, employs its 'blind' medium and the metaphor of a continuous loop of recording tape to involve us with a blind woman and three artists who variously fail to 'see'. Looping back through several periods of time to 1914 and then forward again, this piece combines a murder mystery, a love story, and an inquiry into the meaning of art. The title, which derives from Duchamp's famous *Nude Descending a Staircase*, alludes to all three concerns. The mystery includes a death by falling downstairs; the love story includes a suicidal leap from a window; and the patterned flashbacks themselves, like the images on Duchamp's canvas, are moments in a quasi-cubist analysis of temporal sequence. The artists' debates and their memories of Tzara and Lenin in Zurich will surface again to some extent in *Travesties*. But in *Travesties* the flashbacks are quite different – and not just because Henry

Carr was in fact a consular employee who played in Joyce's production of *The Importance of Being Earnest*, quarrelled with him, and was then travestied by Joyce in the Circe episode of *Ulysses* as a drunken soldier. The mode of *Travesties* itself results from a fusion of Wildean farce, Joycean fiction, Dadaist spontaneous negation, epic theatre, and Shavian dialectic. Balancing an array of radical principles and egocentric procedures, *Travesties* suggests that our 'reality' is at best a shared construction from fragmentary data.

Auden once called *The Importance of Being Earnest* 'perhaps the only purely verbal opera in English'. Wilde's solution there, he said, 'was to subordinate every other element to dialogue for its own sake and create a verbal universe in which the characters are determined by the kinds of things they say, and the plot is nothing but a succession of opportunities to say them'. Stoppard fastens with delight upon that solution, enriches it with Joycean pastiche, parody, and wordplay, and turns it into a medium for a Shavian dialectic that wittily explores the claims of rival principles. (Shaw, we may remember, also insisted on the operatic form of his debates.) In Act One of *Travesties* this dialectic is nearly derailed by the effervescent Tzara, whose serious spoofing infects the play's own style. In Act Two the play swerves in a different direction as Cecily, Nadya, and Lenin nearly turn it into an epic 'teaching play' in the socialist style of Erwin Piscator. The precariously balanced result manages to extend Wilde's achievement, pay tribute to Joyce's artistic faith, acknowledge the power that resides in both Tzara's levity and Lenin's gravity, and offer a more iridescent display of multiple roles and visions than occurs even in Shaw's *Man and Superman* and *Heartbreak House*.

According to Peter Wood, Stoppard had thought of

calling this play *Prism* because, through Carr's memory, it views history 'prismatically'. But surely the appeal of that working title was manifold. *Travesties* refracts our approach to history, art, and revolution through the triangular prism of Joyce-Tzara-and-Lenin, refracts it again through Carr's memory, and again through Stoppard's own multifaceted parody. It therefore becomes a model of the indirections by which we must move toward the white light of a truth beyond our full perception or expression. Tzara has his own version of this rainbow effect, the Dada demand for the 'right to urinate in different colours'. 'Each person in different colours at different times, or different people in each colour all the time?' asks Joyce. 'Or everybody multi-coloured every time?' But *Travesties* also bears a whimsically indirect relation to another Prism, the elderly governess in *The Importance of Being Earnest*, who, twenty-eight years before the action of that play, had accidentally switched the baby 'Ernest' and the manuscript of her triple-decker sentimental novel. In *Travesties* that Prism does not appear as a single character. Her baby-and-manuscript switching is echoed by the manuscript-swapping in the Prologue and the dénouement; her role as Cecily's teacher is assumed by the seemingly untravestied Lenin; her fatuous moralising reappears in old Carr's reminiscences; and her name is everywhere an implicit metaphor in a play that has transmuted Wilde's own *Earnest* into a triple-decker didactic farce. A full appreciation of the prismatic shimmer of this role-switching and role-splitting verbal opera requires our shared presence in the theatre. But some spectroscopic analysis may be useful – beginning with the band of light emitted by the ironic travesty of Wilde's play on earnestness.

Act One of *Travesties* recapitulates Act One of *The*

Importance of Being Earnest with varied repetitions that reduce Wilde's high farce to broad absurdity, load it with ironically qualified didacticism, and employ its epigrammatic style for witty assessments of artistic and political doctrine. After Carr-Algy's conversations with Bennett-Lane, Tzara-Jack's first entrance has led to a manic scene of shared limericks that, like the Prologue, declares the characters to be no more than fragments of a collaborative meaning. When Tzara enters for the second time, however, he too is one of Wilde's sophisticated dandies. In this guise he offers a rather persuasive defence of Dada, provokes Carr into a yet more persuasive attack upon Dada, and then abandons all style as he pursues Carr into an absurdly heated argument. Entering for the third time, Tzara comes yet closer to Wilde's plot and dialogue. Speaking of Cecily and Joyce, he establishes the Library as the equivalent of Jack Worthing's house in the country: 'Well, my name is Tristan in the Meierei Bar and Jack in the library, and the ticket was issued in the library'. ('Tristan', we gather, will be this play's coded name for 'Ernest'.) Then, after defining his political agreement and artistic disagreement with Lenin, Tzara erupts once more in a raving defence of anti-art. At this point Gwendolen and Joyce make their second entrance. After Tzara defines his artistic position against that of Joyce, and Joyce defines his political position against that of Tzara and Lenin, Joyce invites Carr to take Algernon's part in the very play that we have, in effect, been watching for some time. When the two retire to discuss the matter, even as Algy and Lady Bracknell retire to discuss the music for her reception, *Travesties* is at last ready for Wilde's scene between Jack and Gwendolen.

Tzara will offer as a tribute to his Gwendolen his own kind of poem, Shakespeare's eighteenth sonnet reshuffled by the hand of chance. Thanks to Stoppard's farcical magic, however, the preliminary conversation between Tzara and Gwendolen is already composed of tags from *Julius Caesar, Hamlet, As You Like It, Much Ado About Nothing, Henry V, Henry IV (Part One), Othello, The Merry Wives of Windsor,* and the thirty-second sonnet. We are therefore prepared to see a collaborative meaning emerge once more from random bits and pieces. When Gwendolen draws the words of 'Shall I compare thee to a summer's day . . .' from Tzara's hat, they have become a free-verse poem of unmistakably phallic excitement. She is prettily flustered; but after the poem's temperature has dropped, she gives Tzara the folder containing what she supposes to be Joyce's manuscript – for this Gwendolen insists on loving not an 'Ernest' or even a 'Tristan' but an admirer of Joyce. As they embrace, Joyce himself returns, now fully identified with the role of Lady Bracknell': 'Rise, sir, from that semi-recumbent posture!' But he is also now fully himself: his interrogation of Tzara proceeds in the catechistic style of the Ithaca episode in *Ulysses.* Indeed, he now becomes a more astonishing conjurer than Tzara as he takes handkerchiefs and flags from his own hat, reduces Tzara to histrionic violence, lectures him on the nature of the artist, and, reaching once more into his hat, pulls out a rabbit.

Carr ends this first act with a warning that he will now tell us how he met Lenin 'and could have changed the course of history etcetera'. And indeed, Act Two begins in a totally different style with Cecily's lecture on Marx and Lenin. That lecture, however, substitutes for the pedagogical scene between Cecily and Prism that opens Act Two of *The Importance of Being Earnest.* And though the rest of *Travesties* often seems dominated by such didactic material, it also contains an accelerated recapitulation of the second and third acts of Wilde's play. Just as we earlier watched three versions of Tzara-Jack's entrance, so we now watch three versions of Carr-Algy's arrival at the library as 'Tristan Tzara' in pursuit of Cecily. During the first version, he offers his own view of art – a defence of 'Victorian high comedy' against Cecily's charges of bourgeois decadence. During the second, she gives him the folder containing what she supposes to be Lenin's manuscript, and seduces him with her increasingly frenetic defence of revolution – finally appearing to him, and so to us, as a haranguing stripper. During the third version, which echoes the second of Wilde's scenes between Algy and Cecily, the action moves swiftly to a Wildean capitulation ('Ever since Jack told me he had a younger brother who was a decadent nihilist it has been my girlish dream to reform you and love you') and an un-Wildean dive behind the librarian's desk for an embrace. The prickly meeting of the two 'brothers' – Tzara-Jack and Carr-Algy – then comes to us in counterpoint with Nadya's account of Lenin's plan to return to Russia. And after a narrative bridge spoken by old Carr, that counterpoint continues through the narrative and demonstration of Lenin's political and aesthetic views. Soon, however, the strains of Beethoven's 'Appassionata', which have accompanied Nadya's poignant memory of her separation from Lenin during his imprisonment, degenerate absurdly into the mechanical tune of a patter song, 'Mr Gallagher and Mr Shean', and the stage is taken over by socially conscious art of a different kind: a music-hall version of Wilde's upper-class tiff between Cecily and Gwendolen. With heightened artifice and lowered social tone, Stoppard's young ladies translate the elaborately pseudo-polite insults of Wilde's dialogue into neatly rhymed stanzas.

117

In its closing moments, *Travesties* briskly alludes to Act Three of *The Importance of Being Earnest*. Like their counterparts at the beginning of that act, Stoppard's Cecily and Gwendolen have 'just one question' to put to their young men; but this question is about the manuscripts they have given Tzara and Carr to read, and it leads directly into the dénouement. The left-wing Tzara rejects Lenin's manuscript (which he thinks to be Joyce's) as 'unreadable'; the aesthete Carr rejects Joyce's (which he thinks to be Lenin's) as the work of a 'madman'. Their verdicts, though demonstrating to us their political and aesthetic incompetence, pose for the couples an 'insuperable barrier' of 'intellectual differences'. But with Joyce's arrival all is resolved. In Wilde's play, Lady Bracknell thunders: 'Prism, where is that baby?' In Stoppard's, Joyce thunders: 'Miss Carr, where is the missing chapter?' And he alludes, of course, to a chapter of *Ulysses* that does in fact recount through parody and pastiche the birth of a baby. Now, in accord with the Scribean conventions already burlesqued by Wilde, the lovers swiftly untie the knots of misunderstanding, swap folders, embrace, and tie the knots of love with a brief dance.

In the coda old Carr returns to admit, at Cecily's insistence, his most flagrant distortions of history, and to leave us with a rather futile moral:

> I learned three things in Zurich during the war. I wrote them down. Firstly, you're either a revolutionary or you're not, and if you're not, you might as well be an artist as anything else. Secondly, if you can't be an artist, you might as well be a revolutionary.
>
> I forget the third thing.

Though his speech is partly cribbed from the end of *Dogg's Our Pet*, its circle of antitheses and forgotten 'third thing' aptly sum up a play that is yet more elaborately and ironically symmetrical than *The Importance of Being Earnest.* For Stoppard as for Wilde, the foundation of style is a paradoxical antithesis. And as Gwendolen says in *The Importance of Being Earnest,* 'In matters of grave importance, style, not sincerity, is the vital thing'. Though Gwendolen's stylishness is absurdly pretentious, both Wilde and Stoppard would agree with her remark. Both know that style permits a critique of the self-deceptions enjoyed by those who think themselves either sincere or stylish. Both also know that a counterpoint of eccentric styles can illuminate what is central. What Wilde called his 'trivial play for serious people' therefore sparkles with epigrammatic exposures of our folly. And *Travesties*, more brazenly trivial and more insistently serious, uses its symmetries not only to speed up the farce but also to engage at length the antithetical doctrines that have shaped modern art and politics. Carr's forgotten 'third thing' ought ideally to be some synthesis of those doctrines, more genuinely radical than they because more adequate to our scrappy reality. If you cannot be a revolutionary like Lenin, or an artist like Joyce, or a revolutionary anti-artist like Tzara, and if you do not want to be a philistine aesthete like Carr, might you not find such a synthesis of genuine importance? But no doubt that is why Stoppard has allowed it to remain the implicit dialectical burden of this prismatic play.

Central to that dialectic in Act One are the ironic travesties of Tzara and Joyce, who enter here as the symbolic (and, to a large extent, actual) progenitors of the double tradition of modernism in the arts. From Tzara, who was a founder of Dada, later an important surrealist, and finally a dedicated Communist poet and man of letters, descends the subversive tradition of 'anti-art' that has emphasised the spontaneous, absurd, and often socially provocative gesture, howl, or happening. From Joyce, the author of those meta-texts *Ulysses* and *Finnegans Wake,* descends the formalist tradition of 'art' that has emphasised the long-meditated, comprehensive, seemingly apolitical, and labyrinthine artifice. The opposition of the two men, however, is complicated by the fact that each was committed to his own poetic dialectic of continual contradiction – as *Travesties* itself makes clear.

Easily the most captivating character on stage, Tzara is by turns a Rumanian eccentric, a replica of Jack Worthing, a sardonic social critic, a self-consciously outrageous narcissist, and a whirlwind of passionately irreverent and amusing deconstruction. 'I am sick of cleverness,' he says, echoing Jack Worthing with a difference. 'The clever people impose a design on the world and when it goes calamitously wrong they call it fate. In point of fact, everything is Chance, including design.' For Tzara, cleverness 'has been exploded, along with so much else, by the war'. Like the Hemingway of *A Farewell to Arms*, he rejects the sophistry that sanctifies mass murder with the rhetoric of *'patriotism, duty, love, freedom'*. 'Words are taken to stand for opposite facts, opposite ideas. That is why anti-art is the art of our time.' His moral and political outrage wins our sympathy, and his hyperbolic attack on Joyce has a Shavian vigour and finesse:

Your art has failed. You've turned literature into a religion and it's as dead as all the rest, it's an overripe corpse and you're cutting fancy figures at the wake. It's too late for geniuses. Now we need vandals and desecrators, simple-minded demolition men to smash centuries of baroque subtlety, to bring down the temple, and thus finally, to reconcile the shame and the necessity of being an artist!

Nevertheless, we cannot take this versatile opponent of clever corruption at his own assessment. His arguments draw their rhetorical force from the Wildean and Shavian styles in which they have been dressed. His histrionic presence is effective mainly because he is enmeshed, like Shaw's Jack Tanner or Joyce's Stephen Dedalus, in a network of literary parallels and dramatic oppositions. And his aleatory verses have meaning for us primarily because Stoppard has transformed them with Joycean word-play. The complex Tzara therefore gains our assent as one term in a yet more complex dialectic, through which we can see art being forged even from the scraps of absurdism and anti-art.

The explicit proponent of such magic in *Travesties* is Joyce himself, a no less multiple but somewhat less appealing character. He seems at different moments the incarnate spirit of the limerick, a tyrannical Aunt Augusta, an aloof and apolitical artist, a brazen Irishman, the catechistic voice of *Ulysses*, and a flashy conjurer. In a speech added at Peter Wood's urging but later regarded by Stoppard as most important, Joyce says to Tzara: 'An artist is the magician put among men to gratify – capriciously – their urge for immortality'. After he recalls Homer's transmutation of a Greek merchant into Ulysses, 'the wanderer, the most human, the most complete of all heroes – husband, father, son, lover, farmer, soldier, pacifist, politician, inventor, and adventurer,' he concludes: 'It is a theme so overwhelming that I am almost afraid to treat it. And yet I with my Dublin Odyssey will double that immortality, yes by God *there's* a corpse that will dance for some time yet and *leave the world precisely as it finds it* . . . .' Joyce is no doubt right, from the play's point of view, concerning his own achievement. Tzara has said contemptuously that Gwendolen 'is so innocent she does not stop to wonder what possible book could be derived from reference to Homer's *Odyssey* and the Dublin Street Directory for 1904'. But that book, which transmutes fragments of art and life into a multi-faceted and quasi-eternal object, is now being imitated by a play that is itself derived from reference to Wilde's *The Importance of Being Earnest* and accounts of events in Zurich about 1917. Nevertheless, Joyce is not an unqualified spokesman for *Travesties*; nor is Tzara simply incorporated here into a Joycean artifact. The play joins Tzara in distrusting Joyce's subordination of the kinetic to the static, and of politics to art. Its style in Act One has sympathetically lent itself to Tzara's own explosive spontaneity; and it admits in Act Two that a dialectical art must also listen to the voices of dialectical history and politics. Asking us to keep moving towards a yet more adequate understanding of the relations between art and life, it now yields the stage for a time to Lenin – and to a Leninist mode of theatre.

Reviewers have often complained that the Lenin episodes in Act Two are simply expository, that their documentary realism is at odds with the notion of travesty, that they have no relation to *The Importance of Being Earnest*, or that they cannot plausibly be included in Carr's memory. What has happened here to the play's action, tone, structure, and point of view? Stoppard himself has admitted that Cecily's opening lecture might well be shortened and that the character of Lenin on stage may elicit more sympathy from us than his contradictory statements could justify. The main objections to Act Two, however, suggest the reviewers' failure to perceive the radical dialectic to which *Travesties* is committing itself and us.

On returning to our seats after the intermission, we may be surprised to find Cecily giving us a sober lecture on the history of Marxism. But Act One has already foreshadowed this expository mode in Carr's attempts at a memoir, Bennett's reports on current politics, and the history of Dada that Tzara provides in response to Joyce's interrogation. As the limerick took over an entire scene early in the play, so now the lecture has a turn to dominate Stoppard's stylistic collage. When Cecily begins to tell of Lenin's life in Zurich, however, the lecture modulates into yet another style: that of the epic theatre or 'teaching play' developed by Erwin Piscator in Germany during the 1920s and variously modified by Bertolt Brecht. We see James Joyce and 'Tristan Tzara' (actually Carr in spiffy sartorial disguise) enter the library as Cecily speaks of them; and when Lenin and Nadya arrive and repeat their Russian conversation, Cecily translates it for us, speech by speech. After this pedagogical response to the Prologue of Act One, and after Cecily's farcical and argumentative scene with Carr, Nadya herself comes downstage to address us. We now follow at greater length a teaching play that is complete with narrator, illustrative scenes and speeches, images projected on a screen, and incidental sound effects and music. Should Stoppard have given us instead some travesty of the Lenins as characters out of *The Importance of Being Earnest*? As he knew, that would have been an evasive 'trivialisation' of a formidable political figure. 'It would have been disastrous to Prismize and Chasublize the Lenins,' he said to Ronald Hayman, 'and I believe that

that section saves *Travesties* because I think one's just about *had* that particular Wilde joke at that point.' The Lenins must therefore enter now in opposition not just to Tzara and Joyce but to the entire previous action of *Travesties*. That is why – even though Carr fancies that, if he had not been distracted by Cecily and *Earnest*, he might have prevented Lenin's return to Russia and so aborted the Marxist revolution – it is quite appropriate that the Lenins' story comes from beyond Carr's memory. Act One has not precluded this shift to a more inclusive point of view. Its tricky action could not have been generated entirely by Carr's mind, and it often suggests that every character in *Travesties* is a function of our playful collaborative dialectic. In Act Two that dialectic reaches out to interrogate its antithesis: the alleged importance of being in deadly earnest.

Observing Lenin by way of a sympathetic narrative point of view, we find him to be no self-consciously multiple character like Tzara or Joyce. As a stylist, he defines himself with a wilful simplicity. Cecily has told us: 'Lenin was convinced, like Marx, that history worked dialectically, that it advanced through the clash of opposing forces ...'. But believing himself the vehicle of one force in that materialistic dialectic, Lenin avoids a dialectical understanding of his own consciousness. He is therefore half-blind to his inner contradictions and oblivious of the larger aesthetic and ethical dialectic within which *Travesties* has included him.

Some of Lenin's contradictions, of course, are strategic. Nadya's story of his return to Russia includes three virtually simultaneous but quite different plans, each of which Lenin declares to be absolutely essential. And his own oration of 1905 is a passionately devious defence of the necessity of freedom from freedom:

We want to establish and we shall establish a free press, free not simply from the police, but also from capital, from careerism, and what is more, *free from bourgeois anarchist individualism*! These last words may seem paradoxical or an affront to my audience. Calm yourselves, ladies and gentlemen! Everyone is free to write and say whatever he likes, without any restrictions. *But* every voluntary association, including the party, is also free to expel members who use the name of the party to advocate anti-party views.

We observe other contradictions in Lenin, however, which are inadvertent or unwilled. Nadya recalls this revolutionary's respect for 'Tolstoy's traditional values as an artist', his inability to understand expressionism, futurism, and cubism, his preference for Pushkin over Mayakovsky, his disappointment in a production of Gorki's *The Lower Depths* because of the overacting, and his liking for Chekhov's *Uncle Vanya*. We hear him try to persuade his revolutionary friend Gorki that it was proper to arrest bourgeois intellectuals 'in order to prevent plots which threaten the lives of tens of thousands of workers and peasants'; and, in his final speech, we hear him say of a Beethoven sonata:

I don't know of anything greater than the Appassionata. Amazing, superhuman music. It always make me feel, perhaps naïvely, it makes me feel proud of the miracles that human beings can perform. But I can't listen to music often. It affects my nerves, makes me want to say nice stupid things and pat the heads of those people who while living in this vile hell can create such beauty. Nowadays we can't pat heads or we'll get our hands bitten off. We've got to *hit* heads, hit them without mercy, though ideally we're against doing violence to people . . . Hm, one's duty is infernally hard . . .

Although we must have some sympathy for Lenin's earnest opposition to the ground so variously shared by Tzara, Joyce, and *Travesties* itself, his merciless and self-contradictory violence stands in dark contrast to their irreverent but celebratory freedom. And Nadya's own final memory leaves with us another suggestion of loss or waste. She recalls standing on a particular square of pavement on the Shpalernaya in hope that her imprisoned husband might catch a glimpse of her: 'But he never saw me. Something went wrong. I forget what'. That statement, rather than any declaration of revolutionary confidence, stands in this play as Lenin's epitaph. Carr will soon summarise the gist of his own experience with a similar closing phrase: 'I forget the third thing'. The Lenins' dogged but self-imprisoning commitment, like Carr's slithery avoidance of whatever might damage his ego, has required the repression of something important to a full humanity. Carr had earlier spoken foggily of 'The Imprudence of Being –' . . . and had left the title incomplete because he had lost his grip on the name of the character he did *not* play. Risking imprudence and keeping an iron grip on his own earnestness, Lenin has enacted another kind of relative failure.

Reviewing the New York production of 1975 (also directed by Peter Wood) and praising the play as both 'literary' and 'extraordinarily theatrical', Clive Barnes said: 'It is as iridescent as a rainbow glimpsed in a dirty puddle and almost as surprisingly elusive'. That elusiveness of *Travesties* partly results from its implicit dialectic, which invites us to examine with some sympathy an array of radical principles and outrageously egocentric procedures. Tzara, Joyce, and Lenin shape their scrappy worlds into consciously or unconsciously contradictory syntheses. Stoppard asks us to join him in taking significant scraps of their achievements and enacting our own syntheses, which may differ in precise balance but will no doubt all include something of Tzara's irreverence, Lenin's earnestness, and Joyce's dedication to comic transcendence of history through art. *Travesties* therefore cannot attain the 'still centre of the wheel of war' that Carr remembers Switzerland to have been, or that Joyce's *Ulysses* has since become as a work of art. Rather, it generates among us many buoyantly unstable but collaborative centres of the intellectual war in which Tzara, Joyce, and Lenin have been extreme adversaries.

Such dialectical drama, with its historical expositions, witty diatribes, symmetrical debates, and ironic clashes of opposed but almost equally plausible arguments, may well remind us of *Man and Superman, Major Barbara, Heartbreak House,* and *Saint Joan.* Indeed, *Travesties* also exhibits a Shavian as well as a Joycean wit in its tension between heroic types and their burlesque embodiments. But here as elsewhere it strikes a distinctive note. *Man and Superman* transforms its critical farce into a heroic philosophical dream, and then deflates the dream again to the wry realism of farce. *Heartbreak House* subjects its heroic roles – Lear, Othello, Cordelia – to the acids of a corrosive pessimism. *Ulysses* employs its implicit Homeric archetype to provide both critical and celebratory resonances for the wanderings of a very ordinary Leopold Bloom. *Travesties,* however, finds its heroic types in an earlier generation of modern history and lets them be illuminated, but not annihilated, by the farcical figures to which they may be reduced. 'Travesty' here is a knowingly excessive and inadequate undermining of what retains for us a real though not an absolute aesthetic and ethical value. That is why the play's farcical and ambiguous vision can be finally so affirmative. We want at different moments and for different reasons to say 'Da, da, da!' to Lenin, and 'Dada dada dada dada' with Tzara, and 'yes, I said yes' with old Cecily as she unknowingly echoes Joyce's *Molly Bloom*.

Any analysis of the play's iridescence, however, runs the risk of attending to its major historical figures at the expense of Henry Carr, who is far more than the bumbling quasi-begetter of a dialectic that is quite beyond him. In the theatre he is also the living centre of the play – and compellingly so if played by an actor as impressive as John Wood, for whose special talents Stoppard conceived the role. Reviewing the New York production, T. E. Kalem said that Wood 'shifts between his two roles, and two ages of man, with breathtaking ease'. Clive Barnes praised him as not only a 'great' but a 'surprising' actor. 'He takes enormous risks, and wins enormous wages. He takes the audience into his confidence and repays them with leers and chuckles, swoops of voice, and sudden frozen gestures of the body, that sear the memory.' Howard Kissel said that he 'gives the most brittle verbal pyrotechnics the richest, most sensual sounds, as if Stoppard's lines were gorgeous arias'. And Jack Kroll summed up his tribute by describing Wood as 'an insanely gifted actor whose tongue dances and whose body speaks. In a chain-smoking smog of senility or a spat-stamping tattoo of fatuous youth, he is the play incarnate, the most transcendent of travesties'.

Henry Carr is, of course, one term in the dialectic that he sets in motion but fails to understand: a philistine narcissist who can produce neither art, nor anti-art, nor revolution. But as Wood's performance made brilliantly clear, he is also a travesty of ourselves. Living in the unstable and problematic world of time even as he tries to invent a fixed image of the past, Carr fluctuates between trying on historical costumes and requiring the figures of history to wear the costumes his own scrappy imagination dreams up. Perhaps *Travesties* asks us above all to enjoy – and through that enjoyment to purge ourselves of – a Henry Carr who seems to be each of us, at least in our more pretentious and evasive moments, as we try to make meaning out of our lives.

7

Language, Lunacy and Light

Reacting against the 'theatricality' of *Jumpers* and *Travesties,* Stoppard said in 1974 to Ronald Hayman: 'What I'd like to write now is something that takes place in a whitewashed room with no music and no jumping about, but which is a literary piece – so that the energy can go into the literary side of what I do'. But two years later he was questioning the 'literary' as much as the 'theatrical'. He had now 'done a little joke play rather quickly' for Ed Berman and 'a piece to go with an orchestra' for André Previn, was currently working on a screenplay of Nabokov's *Despair* for Rainer Fassbinder, and expressed to Hayman his great admiration for J. B. Priestley's 'sheer craftsmanship'. Watching *The Linden Tree* on television, he found himself wanting to write a conservative play about a middle-class family. 'I felt I was sick of flashy mind-projections speaking in long, articulate, witty sentences about the great abstractions.' Having promised Michael Codron a play, he thought of it as 'a chance to write my West End play, to write *The Linden Tree* or the *Rattigan Version'*.

It is easy to understand Stoppard's feeling that he had reached the end of one line of development, that he could not improve on *Travesties* if he were 'to write that kind of play in that kind of idiom'. It is harder to believe that his talents could ever be fully engaged by an array of more limited challenges, or to see why he would want to imitate Priestley or Terence Rattigan as he had once imitated Bolt and Miller. In 1973 he had told Janet Watts, however, that he 'would like ultimately before being carried out feet first to have done a bit of absolutely everything'. And in 'Ambushes for the Audience' he had warned: 'I'm a professional writer – I'm for hire if you like – as well as being someone who pursues his own path in his writing'. Since *Travesties,* those two roles have often merged as Stoppard has continued to extend his stylistic range – and ours.

Since *Travesties* he has also been increasingly concerned about the denial of civil liberties in Eastern Europe. In 1975, as a member of the Committee Against Psychiatric Abuse, an arm of Amnesty International, he marched in protest against the treatment of Soviet dissidents. In 1976 he met Victor Fainberg, who had been exiled from the USSR after five years in prison-hospitals for having protested the invasion of Czechoslovakia. In February 1977, as a member of the International Committee for the Support of the Principles of Charter 77, he wrote to *The Times* about the harassment of Vaclav Havel by the Czech government. During the same month, he visited Moscow and Leningrad, reporting on the visit in *The Sunday Times.* Then in July he went to Czechoslovakia, where he met Vaclav Havel and Pavel Kohout and gained a first-hand acquaintance with their political situation, which he described in *The New York Review of Books*. During the same period, Stoppard's various dramatic projects began to reflect these concerns.

Reviewers have written with approval or dismay of a newly 'serious' Stoppard, who has diluted or sacrificed his distinctive qualities in pursuit of simpler styles and more narrowly political themes. It is true that in his recent work the structures are less elaborate, the implications less rich, and the sallies of wit no longer so incessant. But Stoppard was never an absurdist or a mere showman, and his basic assumptions remain the same. Even when seeming ambivalent on almost every issue, Stoppard's work has always implied a firm belief in freedom of expression. Now, in meeting his commitments to Berman, Previn, and Codron, and in urging the cause of free speech, he has made yet more explicit his faith that collaborative play, as it explores our slippery language and potentially murderous lunacy, can both lighten and enlighten our condition.

First performed in April 1975, as a lunch-hour production at Inter-Action's Almost Free Theatre (and later moved to the Arts Theatre for a long run), the one-act combination of *Dirty Linen* and *New-Found-Land* was commissioned by the expatriate director, Ed Berman, for a series ('The American Connection') to celebrate his British naturalisation during that American Bicentennial year. *Dirty Linen* treats as farce a situation that arises easily enough in London or Washington when our political, sexual, and journalistic games collide. The political game, as played here by members of a Select Committee on Moral Standards in Public Life, meeting in the tower of Big Ben, requires the continual pretence that one is engaged in a complex task of national importance. '. . . I think it is fair to say', says McTeazle as he instructs the Committee's new secretary:

> that this Committee owes its existence to the determination of the Prime Minister to keep his House in order, whatever the cost in public ridicule, whatever the consequences to people in high places, and to the fact that the newspapers got wind of what was going on.

What is going on is the sexual game played by these same MPs, which seems to require their going to bed as often as possible with a certain 'Mystery Woman'. 'This Committee,' McTeazle continues:

> was set up at the time when the good name of no fewer than 21 Members of Parliament was said to have been compromised. Since then rumour has fed on rumour and we face the possibility that a sexual swath has passed through Westminster claiming the reputations of, to put no finer point upon it, 119 members. Someone is going through the ranks like a lawn-mower in knickers.

But that 'someone' (as we immediately guess, and as McTeazle already knows) is none other than the shapely, commonsensical, but nymphomaniacal secretary that he is now addressing, Maddie Gotobed. The journalistic game, of course, requires that all such dirty linen be exposed, ostensibly for the public good but really for the competitive advantage of individual journalists. 'They're not writing it for the people,' says Maddie, 'they're writing it for the writers writing it on the other papers. . . . The *pictures* are for the people.'

But anyone who enjoys this farce can hardly condescend to 'the people', and Stoppard's theatre game therefore insists that the pictures are also for *us*. Whenever an MP is transfixed by a pin-up photo of Maddie in a tabloid, the action freezes and a bright flash catches her on stage in a provocative pose. Other sight-gags involve the members' accidental exposure of their own dirty linen (knickers and briefs pop up everywhere) and their progressive stripping of Maddie herself. Their approval of a windily defensive report is resisted for some time by a late arrival, the proper Mr French. But when they adjourn for ten minutes for a voting call from the floor of the House, the nearly stripped Maddie asks his help: 'Could you show me the ladies cloakroom'. And after the adjournment (during which we watch *New-Found-Land* take place in the same committee room), French has reversed himself. Explaining that Maddie has 'poured out her heart' to him, he offers a substitute report embodying the position that she had earlier urged on the Committee. 'All you need,' she had said, 'is one paragraph saying that MPs have got just as much right to enjoy themselves in their own way as anyone else, and Fleet Street can take a running jump.' French's own language, of course, is loftier: 'this principle is not to be sacrificed to that Fleet-Street stalking-horse masquerading as a sacred cow labelled "The People's Right to Know" '. But after the vote he wipes his brow with the knickers that, in the play's opening moment, we had watched Maddie put on. And Big Ben, which has been punctuating their lunacy with its deafening vibrations, strikes the quarter hour.

Visually and topically, this play may be the 'undergraduate satire' that one New York reviewer, Martin Gottfried, declared it. (Another reviewer, Walter Kerr, thought it 'slovenly' and 'altogether intolerable'.) Stoppard himself was rather deprecatory: 'My director thinks he's got a profound comment on British society,' he told Robert Semple. 'What he really has is a knickers farce'. As French's strained rhetoric suggests, however, Stoppard's theatre game has also a more serious (though not at all solemn) interest. It uses low farce as a field within which to explore our chronic intoxication with language. The opening dialogue signals that intention: McTeazle and Cocklebury-Smythe speak for quite some time without using a word of English, being content to toss off French, Latin, and Italian clichés. We then follow an astonishing sequence of linguistic leaps, slithers, switch-backs, and catalogues. The MPs complicate their usual triple-lingo (bureaucratic obfuscation, high-flying rhetoric, and street talk) with punning innuendoes ('the papers naturally resort to sticking their noses into upper reaches of top drawers looking for hankie panties, etcetera'), Freudian slips ('why don't you have a quick poke, peek, in the Members' Bra – or the cafeteria'), and anxiously romantic admonitions to Maddie that, when interrupted, slide smoothly in and out of an allusion to Dickens or a definition of 'quorum'. As the chairman says when defending the football jargon Maddie has introduced: 'The terminology of committee practice is in a constant state of organic change, Mr French. If you can't keep up you'll be of no use to us.' Varied by rapid-fire parliamentary formalities and slow-motion dictation of angry debate, the dialogue skips onward through impertinent retorts ('What is that?' 'Pair of briefs.' 'What are they doing there?' 'It's a brief case'), pertinent misunderstandings ('Do you use Greggs or do you favour the Pitman method?' 'I'm on the pill'), and tongue-twisting anti-mnemonic refrains ('Never at Claridges, Coq d'Or, Crockford's with Cockie. Never at Claridges, Coq d'Or, Crockford's with Cockie') to Maddie's potentially endless confessional chant:

. . . I was at the Poule au Pot and the Coq au Vin and the Côte d'Azur and the Foo Luk Fok and the Grosvenor House and Luigi's and Lacy's and the Light of India with Johnny and Jackie and Jerry and Joseph and Jimmy, and in the Berkeley, Biancis, Blooms, and Muldoons with Micky and Michael and Mike and Michelle . . . .

We seem by now such stuff as language is made of – and *New-Found-Land* cuts in to make just that point. Two Home Office types, one very old and deaf and the other very young, enter the room to consider an application for citizenship, the visual and verbal language of which – an American, a beard, a farm in Kentish Town, £10·50 a week, interests in publishing, buses, theatre – suggests to the elder nothing but disadvantages: '. . . are we supposed to tell the Minister that he's just the sort of chap the country needs?' Indeed, each official is turned on only by his own style of language. The elder has told with relish but imperfect comprehension a tedious anecdote from his childhood about meeting Lloyd George (who, we gather, must have been playing his own sexual game); and the younger now delivers, as his partner dozes off, an even lengthier bravura celebration of a trans-American train-trip (in verbiage that sounds as if Thomas Wolfe had been hired to write a travel brochure). When *Dirty Linen* resumes, we are prepared to admit that national styles, like those of occupations and individuals, are mainly composed of pretentious nonsense and inadvertent self-disclosure. And yet, when the Home Secretary whips out his pen to sign Ed Berman's application after all ('One more American can't make any difference'), we wish the new Britisher well. The light shed by this playful linguistic lunacy has been more than adequate to the occasion.

Language, Lunacy and Light

Every Good Boy Deserves Favour leads us into a much subtler pattern of lunacy, not only amusing but also ominous and poignant. The title, a mnemonic aid used in teaching children the lines in the treble staff, here expands in meaning to evoke a society based on a rigid notion of harmonious order, its systems of miseducation and injustice, and its attempts to use paternal responsibility as a weapon against conscientious dissent. Not a 'play' but a 'piece for actors and orchestra', with music by André Previn, *EGBDF* was first performed at the Royal Festival Hall on 1 July 1977, by the Royal Shakespeare Company under Trevor Nunn's direction and the 100-piece London Symphony Orchestra conducted by Previn. Recast, and with a 32-piece orchestra, it had an extended run at the Mermaid Theatre. In the summer of 1979 Stoppard himself followed Nunn's production concept in directing it, with an 81-piece orchestra conducted by David Gilbert, at the Metropolitan Opera in New York.

Despite the verbal playfulness in its title and its form, *EGBDF* contains only one insistent punster, an exuberant, sardonic, and sometimes aggressively paranoid triangle-player named Alexander Ivanov, who conducts an imaginary orchestra in the mental hospital to which he has been confined. (John Wood played this role with dazzling virtuosity in the first performance.) Ivanov's lunacy does not obscure from us his talents: his inventive language is pure Stoppard, and his orchestra, which we can usually hear, plays music worthy of Previn. In accord, no doubt, with bureaucratic logic, the Colonel in charge of what is really a hospital-prison has also assigned to Ivanov's cell another inmate bearing the same name. Called Alexander in the script, though not on stage, the second Alexander Ivanov seems the psychological and stylistic opposite of the first. (Ian McKellen played the role with moving restraint in the first performance, and Eli Wallach brought to it a more obstinate passion in New York.) A laconic man of plain sense, firm will, and quiet irony, he tells how he was imprisoned here for doing something 'really crazy': he had said, truly enough, that a friend of his had been put in prison for saying that sane people are being put in mental hospitals. He now refuses to eat, tells his story with an algebraic reticence, and composes affectionate letters in doggerel verse to his little son, Sacha. That son, the third Alexander Ivanov in the insistently triangular pattern of this piece, is a rather stubborn but vulnerable child who refuses to accept the skewed logic and ethics that ostensibly justify his father's imprisonment, and who also plays both triangle and drum with wilful passion in his school's percussion band.

The three Ivanovs are counterpointed against three functionaries who render the lunatic style of a system that not only denies human freedom but also distorts art and thought. The Doctor is an anxious conformist, skilled in psychoanalytic put-downs, who plays the violin in a real orchestra. The Teacher is an authoritarian who responds to the definitions in Sacha's geometry book with her own self-contradictory definitions of 'antisocial malcontents', and who also directs the percussion band. And the Colonel in charge of this hell of repressed creativity and suppressed language is a semanticist and Doctor of Philology whose reputed 'genius' is hard to distinguish from stupidity.

As Stoppard has said in a note to the published script, his portrayal of a rigidly orchestrated society draws on the experiences of Victor Fainberg and Vladimir Bukovsky. Alexander's account of his treatment in the Leningrad Special Psychiatric Hospital is taken from Fainberg's article in *Index Against Censorship*, 'and there are other borrowings from life, such as the doctor's comment, ''Your opinions are your symptoms" '. This Russian perversion of psychiatry has also been described in *A Question of Madness* by Zhores Medvedev, a scientist who had been diagnosed as having 'incipient schizophrenia' with 'paranoid delusions of reforming society'. Such coercive defining of abnormality, however, is not just a Russian temptation. *EGBDF* makes that point obliquely through the first Ivanov, who, in a mad-scene somewhat reminiscent of *King Lear*, becomes a hyperbolic image of the repressive mania of which we are all capable. Earlier scenes have shown how language, music, logic, geometry, politics, and ethics are all distorted by the Doctor's and the Teacher's authoritarian sanity, which Sacha has parodied in his own rebellious definitions: 'A triangle is the shortest distance between three points', and 'A plane area bordered by high walls is a prison not a hospital'. Now sitting in the Doctor's chair, Ivanov terrifies Sacha with raving axioms that travesty Euclid, the Declaration of Independence, and Matthew 19:24 ('Everyone is equal to the triangle', 'It is easier for a sick man to play the triangle than for a camel to play the triangle'), and that build to this screaming climax: 'What is the Golden Rule? . . . A line *must be drawn*!' (The geometrical wit of Ivanov's summation brightly transforms such middle-class wisdom as that of Shaw's Johnny Tarleton in *Misalliance*: 'You can draw a line and make other chaps toe it. That's what I call morality.')

Perhaps the ultimate question implicit in *EGBDF* is simply this: On what authority do we decide not to treat our neighbour with love or respect but to define him as 'mentally ill' and lock him up in a plane area bordered by high walls? A good many social scientists, of course, have recently explored that question – among them Erving Goffman (in *Asylums*), Thomas Szasz (in *The Myth of*

Mental Illness and other works), and Michel Foucault (in *Madness and Civilization*). But since Pirandello, many playwrights have also explored it; and *EGBDF* brings especially to mind Pinter's *The Birthday Party* (with its pseudo-psychiatric interrogation of Stanley), Orton's *What the Butler Saw* (with its vision of a mental institution run by the stark raving sane), and N. F. Simpson's *One Way Pendulum* (in which a strangely withdrawn young musician conducts his weighing machines in the 'Hallelujah Chorus'). But Stoppard himself has always been fascinated by the languages of withdrawal, hysteria, and rebellion. And the 'insane' Alexander Ivanovs belong to that line of antithetical twins (the jailor and prisoner of *The Gamblers*, Lord Malquist and Mr Moon, Guildenstern and Rosencrantz, Archie Jumper and George Moore, Tzara and Lenin) through whom he has long been defining and redefining his bipolar world: flashy wit and plodding earnestness, narcissism and sympathy, art and politics.

The semi-musical form of *EGBDF* emerges from problems playfully invited and solved. Previn had first suggested that Stoppard write a narration around which he could build an orchestral piece. Stoppard responded almost at once with the more original and more genuinely collaborative notion of a piece for actors and orchestra. The risks were obvious: a symphony orchestra on stage might easily overpower the actors, the music might dilute or impede the action, and the total effect might seem unwieldy or pretentious. For the most part, those risks have been avoided or turned to advantage. The orchestra here seems a virtuoso actor: it delights the audience with its mimed passages, its various responses to its lunatic conductor, and its parody of the Doctor's movements; it plays a threatening nightmare when Alexander sleeps and a bit of Tschaikovsky's '1812 Overture' when he confronts Ivanov over Tolstoy's *War and Peace*; it suggests through pastiche of Prokoviev and Shostakovitch the controlling Soviet ethos; and it becomes the percussion band in which Sacha bangs away without regard for the written notes. Conversely, the actors often seem individual instruments: they enter into dialogues with the orchestra and antiphonal 'duologues' with each other, and Alexander's longest speech is scored and lit as a solo. Though Previn's somewhat cinematic and perhaps 'overscored' music does tend to blur chronology and suspend the action, those effects are appropriate in the limbo of an asylum or prison. And though the slender dramatic line may hold its own rather precariously against a full symphony orchestra on stage, that effect too is thematic. As a massive visible and audible environment, the orchestra renders the inner and outer forces that have already dominated four characters and threaten to overwhelm the other two. At the Metropolitan Opera the orchestra nearly filled a bank of red-carpeted elevations that led up to a red-draped back wall. Within that ominously formal and often darkened space were the three small and separately lit playing areas – the prisoners' cell (in front of the podium), the Doctor's office (on a platform behind the string basses), and the schoolroom (on a platform behind the violins) – and through it Sacha finally wandered in search of his father.

Stoppard's stylistic counterpoint interweaves the uneasily comic theme of the paranoid Ivanov, the heroic theme of the firmly resistant Alexander, and the poignant theme of the vulnerable Sacha, developing them through many symmetries, contrasts, and incremental repetitions. Encounters between Sacha and the Teacher, Ivanov and the Doctor, and Alexander and the Doctor stress both analogies and differences among the three patterns of resistance to authority. These dovetail with scenes relating Ivanov to Alexander, Alexander to Sacha, and then Sacha to Ivanov, which render conflicts or misunderstandings among the resisters themselves. After Sacha's terrifying encounter with Ivanov, the sequence climaxes in the 'duologue' between Alexander's doggerel letters and Sacha's sung pleas that his father give up his hunger strike, lie to the authorities, and live.

Because Alexander's resistance cannot be broken even by that appeal and the authorities cannot allow him to die, a 'logical impasse' occurs, which requires of the Colonel (and the playwright) a surprising strategy. In a grandiose sky-blue uniform, the Colonel makes a long and impressive entrance accompanied by full organ music. Brushing interruptions aside, he asks each Alexander Ivanov a question appropriate to the other. Because Ivanov does not think sane people are put in mental hospitals and Alexander has no orchestra, both can be released at once. Some critics have questioned the realism of this sly bureaucratic confusion; but the style of the Colonel's entrance has already declared him a *deus ex machina*; and his decision, like the release of MacHeath in the 'rewritten' ending of Gay's *The Beggar's Opera,* is also the author's own ironic acknowledgement of our desires. Stoppard's ambiguous finale expands this irony in another mode. After the Teacher, the Doctor, and Ivanov have joined the orchestra, Sacha meets his father downstage and then runs ahead of him through the orchestra up a central aisle – and (in the Stoppard-Nunn production) toward a shaft of light. Reaching the top, he sings again, as if Alexander had not yet been released: 'Papa, don't be crazy! Everything can be all right!' Alexander calls to him; and the boy repeats his optimistic refrain, which echoes a sentence earlier used by both Alexander and the Teacher.

Beneath his innocence and insistence, we feel a darkness that *Every Good Boy Deserves Favour* does not pretend to dispel.

Though simple in outline, *EGBDF* is remarkably complex in its inner form. Reviewing the New York production, Mel Gussow complained that the metaphor of the 'dissident' as a 'discordant note' in society works for the theatrical but not the musical part of the evening. 'What if all the triangles, piccolos, cellos, and kettle drums went blissfully in their own direction without benefit of score or conductor? The result would not be dissidence or dissonance but cacaphony.' But nowhere has the piece suggested through its carefully limited analogy any endorsement of such rigid and extreme alternatives. It has clearly differentiated Ivanov's unwilled rebellion, which produces music audible only to himself and us, from Sacha's wilful tantrums, which do indeed produce cacaphony, and both from Alexander's sober ethical commitment, which is quite consistent with a freely collaborative social order. Nor is music here essentially tyrannical. *EGBDF* recognises, of course, that any constructive or healing order can be perverted and misused by those who anxiously shout that 'a line *must be drawn*!' But its own playful and collaborative harmonies – both theatrical and musical – illuminate for us the social lunacy that turns music (or language, or psychiatry, or geometry, or the Gospel) into a tyranny from which a conscientious man can only dissent.

Professional Foul, a television play of September 1977, dramatises a similar political situation in a much more conventional form. But it brings to that popular medium a subtle exploration of a problem posed in *Jumpers*: How can we justify ethical action in a time distrustful of all claims in behalf of absolute values and sceptical of language itself? Anderson, a distinguished but diffident Cambridge professor, is attending a philosophical congress in Prague, where he is slated to give a paper on 'Ethical Fictions as Ethical Foundations'. He has less interest in the paper, however, than in his slightly 'naughty' plan to take in the World Cup qualifying football match between England and Czechoslovakia. He is approached by a former student, Pavel Hollar, now barred from Czech academic life, who has just completed his doctoral thesis on the source of the collective ethic in the individual ethic. Hollar partly justifies his argument that individuals have inherent rights by observing the behaviour of his own son, Sacha. (The position is less naïve than it might seem: the psychologist Jerome Kagan now argues in his recent book, *The Second Year,* that nineteenth-century thinkers were correct in holding that the child has an innate sense of morality.) When Hollar asks Anderson to smuggle the thesis back to England, Anderson refuses: 'I mean it would be bad manners, wouldn't it?' He also rejects, as inconsistent with Hollar's own ethics, a suggestion that Hollar might hide the thesis somewhere in his luggage.

The next afternoon, intending to return the thesis on his way to the game, Anderson finds that Hollar has been arrested and that police are searching the Hollar apartment. Detained during the search, which ostensibly turns up some illegal dollars, Anderson can only listen to the game on the radio. That night he meets with Mrs Hollar and Sacha in a park. Serving as his mother's translator and also as a moral agent in his own right, Sacha warns Anderson that Hollar has really been arrested for signing Charter 77 and that Anderson himself will surely be searched at the airport. When Anderson returns to the hotel he finds that another philosopher, McKendrick – who has seemed more interested in women and jazz than in his professed Marxism, and whose own paper argues that ethical principles reverse themselves at the 'catastrophe point' – has become drunk and is self-righteously attacking an English football player for having committed a deliberate or 'professional' foul that afternoon in the hope of preventing a Czech goal. These events lead Anderson to reverse his own position. He had previously remonstrated with McKendrick: 'What need have you of moral courage when your principles reverse themselves so conveniently?' But now he answers his own question by committing one act that is unmannerly and another that is both illegal and unethical. He writes a new paper on the conflict between individual and community rights, in effect a critique of totalitarianism, and insists on presenting it to his session. (The chairman finally silences him by faking a fire alarm.) He also hides Hollar's thesis in McKendrick's luggage, unbeknownst to McKendrick himself, and so smuggles it out of the country. On discovering that he has been so used, McKendrick is predictably outraged; but Anderson disarmingly grants that his colleague might be right: 'Ethics is a very complicated business'. In fact, Anderson has committed his own 'professional foul' for the sake of freedom.

His new position, which requires him to break lesser rules for the sake of an ultimate concern, contrasts not only with McKendrick's self-indulgence and self-righteousness but also with the absolute ethics and the naïveté of young Chetwyn, a neo-Thomist who has been active on behalf of persecuted professors and is now caught when trying to carry out some letters to Amnesty International and the United Nations. A fourth philosopher, an American named Stone who pedantically argues for an unambiguous 'logical language' but is quite unaware of his own verbal ambiguity and non-verbal rudeness, seems absurdly remote from any ethical discourse or action. Commenting reluctantly on Stone's paper, Anderson observes that 'language is not the only level of human communication, and perhaps not the most important level. Whereof we cannot speak, thereof we are by no means silent'. That witty reversal of a famous sentence near the end of Wittgenstein's *Tractatus Logico-Philosophicus* points to Anderson's new ethical ground. His own paper argues (against linguistic philosophy, and with Hollar's help) that we have an obligation to regard our ethical fictions as if they were true, and that the fiction of 'natural justice' is 'an attempt to define a sense of rightness which is not simply derived from some other utterance elsewhere'. Playing his new role with moral courage and finesse, Anderson justifies the light of his conscience with an axiom that, strange as it may seem, underlies all of Stoppard's own linguistic jugglery: 'There is a sense of right and wrong which precedes utterance'.

Politics and ethics also enter Stoppard's 'West End play', which was first directed by Peter Wood at the Phoenix Theatre in November 1978, starring Diana Rigg as Ruth Carson. *Night and Day* focuses on three newsmen for the *Sunday Globe* who are covering a civil war in Kambawe, a fictitious African country, and also on the frustrated wife of the mine-owner who is trying to manipulate that war to his own advantage. Stoppard's situation updates that in Evelyn Waugh's farcical novel *Scoop* (1933), in which the inexperienced William Boot is sent by *The Beast* to cover the political turmoil in the mineral-rich country of Ishmaelia. In *Night and Day,* President Mageeba seems an Idi Amin who has been educated at the London School of Economics; and Colonel Shimbu's revolution has Soviet backing. But the long-distance arguments between reporter Richard Wagner and his editor about the status of the young special correspondent (and former scab) Jacob Milne recall Boot's own muddled communications with *The Beast* about his employment. Waugh had a good deal of fun with the condensed jargon of radiograms – 'UNPROCEED LAKUWARD' – and Stoppard now has yet more fun with that used on the telex: 'Onpass Wagner. Upstick protest arsewards'. Stoppard acknowledges his debts to Waugh by letting Wagner impudently answer Geoffrey Carson, the owner of Kambawe's copper mines, with an evasive line often used in the offices of *The Beast*: 'Up to a point, Lord Copper'.

Reviewers and critics have often described *Night and Day* as a Shavian debate (about freedom of the press, the dangers to journalism of a closed union shop, and the venality of the newspaper business) that seems strangely subordinate to an irrelevant protagonist. Harold Hobson, for example, called it 'a comparatively straightforward play' that presents a social question 'with the dialectical skill of a Shaw combined with the neat and moving melodramatic cleverness of a Rattigan'. But he found Ruth Carson's presence 'most mysterious', though granting that she was 'played fascinatingly by the regal and Delilahlike Diana Rigg'. When the play arrived in New York in November 1979, directed again by Wood but with Maggie Smith as Ruth, others objected more vigorously to its apparent incoherence. Douglas Watt thought Smith 'divine' in this 'Shavian drawing-room comedy' but was 'not at all sure what the character she plays . . . is doing there'. Howard Kissel, who found the debate tedious, praised her rendering of 'a totally extraneous part'. Walter Kerr wondered whether Stoppard 'is a true dramatist at all'. The Shavian debate 'really takes place in a void', he said. 'Miss Smith's romantic life doesn't influence the argument in the least. Nor does the argument measurably affect the politics of Kambawe'. Even Jack Kroll, who understood that Stoppard was experimenting with conventional forms, thought the play 'didn't hold together'.

The ironic doubleness of *Night and Day* is in fact more Shavian than these comments suggest. (Imagine the difficulties that the tricky and implausible coherence of *Misalliance* or *Heartbreak House* would pose for such reviewers.) Stoppard himself said to Robert Berkvist in 1979:

> The best thing that can happen to a playwright is to discover that two plays he's been thinking about can actually be the same play. That way, with some luck, you can wind up with more than the sum of the two parts. Journalism was an interest of mine, I wanted to write a . . . love story, really, and finally the arcs intersected.

That intersection owes something to Waugh: Ruth Carson presses herself on Jacob Milne somewhat as Kätchen, the commonlaw wife of a German mining engineer, presses herself on William Boot. But Stoppard's double plot also requires a bold contrivance. By a stunning but morally appropriate coincidence, the stranger with whom Ruth had spent a night in London is the Richard Wagner who turns up at her home in Kambawe because his editor has learned that Geoffrey Carson owns a telex. A roughly similar coincidence is the brilliant basis for Noel Coward's *Private Lives,* but we may think this one at odds with the 'realism' of *Night and Day.* If so, we should think again not only about this play's frequently farcical tone but also about the fact that it can begin with George Guthrie's nightmare (which we take at first for waking reality) and then swiftly move, when Wagner is mentioned, to inhabit Ruth's point of view as well, through asides underlined by off-stage piano chords from the Beatles' *Help*! Though Stoppard may be too smoothly fulfilling the expectations of his West-End audience, *Night and Day* is no 'realistic' or 'naturalistic' play. The author of *Travesties* had told Kenneth Tynan that 'truth telling writing is as big a lie as the deliberate fantasies I construct. It's based on the fallacy of naturalism'. Far from having decided now to embrace that fallacy, he has shaped an artifice that freely uses naturalism, expressionistic fantasy, farce, melodrama, and debate as complementary perspectives on the 'real'. Through its mixed style the play sets in motion an elaborate mobile of interlocking dualities: day and night, man and woman, 'work' and 'love', life and death, realism and fantasy, the spoken and unspoken, politics and business, pragmatism and idealism, deception and honesty.

The title is already a clue, pointing to the worlds of masculine work (journalism, business, politics) and feminine passion (a bitter substitute here for real work or love), and to the opposites in each. Wood's production announced this doubleness by projecting newspaper headlines on a screen while playing Cole Porter's 'Night and Day'. The play itself uses the photographer Guthrie's day-time nightmare to plunge us at once into the journalistic 'night and day' of 24-hour duty and sharp conflicts. Within seconds the sun has set, jeeplights blind us in the darkness, a helicopter searchlight picks out Guthrie, and a machinegun burst kills him. A few seconds later it is again late afternoon and Guthrie is sleeping in the Carson garden as the telex chatters. During Act One the stage will slowly darken, and then we will see night again suddenly transformed into day – this time the dawn in which Guthrie and Milne leave for Shimbu's headquarters in Malkuangazi. Act Two begins with another dream – now Ruth's night-time day-dream of seducing Milne, a sequence that some incompletely attentive reviewers of the first production confused with waking reality. At about the same time, as we will later learn, Guthrie's nightmare is becoming an off-stage reality for him and Milne: their jeep is fired upon by a machinegun and Milne is killed.

In this chiaroscuro field the journalistic opposites also unfold. The main contrast at first seems that between the partners Guthrie and Wagner: the non-verbal photographer, honest, kind to little Alastair Carson, and courageously willing to accompany Milne on what seems a doomed mission; and the articulate reporter, devious, condescending, and ready to hide even from Guthrie his chance at an interview with Mageeba. But Milne himself provides for Wagner a more telling antithesis. Though seeming a lucky novice and a naïve idealist, he sees through the glib rhetoric of Wagner's trade-unionism and accepts the commercial vacuity of most so-called news only as 'the price you pay' for responsible journalism. He has learned, in fact, to live with the opposites of the fourth estate: 'inside society and yet outside it, with a licence to scourge it and a duty to defend it, night and day . . . .'

Thriving within and upon journalism, the linked opposites of business and politics are writ large in Carson's collaboration with Mageeba, which leads the President to pay a night call in Act Two. Ruth's conflicting passions collide with all of these masculine worlds, illuminating them ironically from outside and inside. (She often seems in effect our woman in Kambawe, an honest if quite private journalist.) Ruth is intelligent but without training or vocation. 'That's the disadvantage of being carried off as a virgin', she says; 'it was years before I discovered I was brighter than most of the people I met. I mean, I could run the mines, Geoffrey, if I knew anything about mining.' She is also passionate but without any commitments. 'I'm not in love with anybody,' she tells Wagner. 'I just like some people a great deal more than I like others ....' But her professed liking for Geoffrey does not prevent her unreciprocated passion for Milne or her later resumption of the affair with Wagner. She seems to be trying to transform her banal social entrapment into a wry version of some Maugham tale of torrid adultery in an isolated outpost of the empire. Her 'unspoken' asides fill her emptiness with obsessive role-playing, spinning self-ironic worlds out of clichés drawn from popular songs and films. Even during the tension of Mageeba's conversation with Carson and Wagner she withdraws to her ironic and guilt-ridden chatter: 'I talk to myself in the middle of a conversation. In fact I talk to myself in the middle of an *imaginary* conversation, which is itself a refuge from some other conversation altogether, frequently imaginary'. And yet her perceptions are penetrating and often quite just. Though Milne's eloquent defence of a free press has helped to arouse her passion, after his death she can put the contrary case in a persuasive diatribe:

I'm not going to let you think he died for free speech and the guttering candle of democracy – crap! Jake died for the product. He died for the women's page, and the crossword, and the racing results, and the heartbreak beauty queens and somewhere at the end of a long list I suppose he died for the leading article too, but it's never worth *that* –

Somewhere in her double mind or broken heart, however, she hopes very much that the truth might be otherwise.

In that debate about the press the final explicit word is the laconic Guthrie's retort to Ruth: 'People do awful things to each other. But it's worse in places where everybody is kept in the dark. It really is. Information is light. Information, in itself, about anything, is light. That's all you can say, really.' As usual, his image is worth a thousand words. The play itself, however, continues with Shavian ambivalence toward its own more intense kind of 'light' – a sardonic darkness. Wagner's response to Milne's death is quite pragmatic: 'There's always other stories, Gigi'. When he learns that his protest against Milne's employment has provoked a strike that blocks his own story on Mageeba from publication, he handles that pragmatically, too: he will telex the story of Milne's death to the provincial paper for which the correspondent had once worked. And when Ruth implies that, however bitterly, she will now return to him, Wagner seems prepared to continue their affair. Though we reserve our intellectual and moral endorsement for the now absent Milne and Guthrie, we sympathise precariously with these self-trapped pragmatists as they settle for each other. Finally, *Night and Day* locates us both outside and inside Ruth's predicament by inviting us to share her imagination of the scene. At the keyboard of the telex, Wagner becomes a piano-player to whose chords Ruth sings Rodgers and Hart's wry lyric, 'The Lady is a Tramp.' But before she can utter that last word, Wagner tears the paper out of the machine and joins her. 'Is that it?' she asks. 'That's it.' And a black-out completes Stoppard's ironic elucidation of our worlds of doubleness.

Stoppard's next play celebrates a light that is almost

indistinguishable from levity itself. *Dogg's Hamlet, Cahoot's Macbeth* was first performed under Ed Berman's direction by his British American Repertory Company at the University of Warwick, Coventry, in May 1979. After it had opened in July for a run at the Collegiate Theatre in London, Jack Kroll declared: 'The incorrigibly playful Stoppard has never been more serious than in this most playful of his works'. When BARC brought *Dogg's Hamlet, Cahoot's Macbeth* to New York in the fall, however, others dismissed it as 'marginal' (Mel Gussow), 'mere conceits' (Douglas Watt), 'ultra-chic noises' (Clive Barnes), and even 'smart-ass' (Christopher Sharp). Nevertheless, Kroll had rightly discerned in this often childlike piece 'Stoppard's unique quality of somehow being ingenious and profound'.

As Ed Berman told Robert Berkvist in September 1979, the Inter-Action Game Method 'postulates that children's games are inherited capacities and that the universality of those games is a keystone of human development – and, most important, the basic instrument by which we learn to create'. Since 1968 Inter-Action had been developing that Game Method into techniques of participatory theatre and many kinds of social action. Working with Berman's troupe in 1971, Stoppard had developed *Dogg's Our Pet*, which uses the miming of pre-linguistic or trans-linguistic games to teach the audience a mildly shocking language composed of ordinary English words. And, like Berman, he was quite prepared to treat children's play and intuition with full seriousness. His most creative adult characters are always remarkably childlike, and in recent plays the children often point to the most admirable human traits. The wilful but loyal and innocent Sacha of *Every Good Boy Deserves Favour* suggests an anti-totalitarian ethos. In *Professional*

Foul another Sacha is regarded by two philosophers as evidence of our innate sense of freedom and justice. Even in *Night and Day* little Alastair Carson, whose parents are busy with their own self-compromising affairs, is appropriately drawn toward the honest and courageous Guthrie. It is initially but not finally surprising that Stoppard could think of combining *Dogg's Our Pet* and its sequel, *The (15 Minute) Dogg's Troupe Hamlet*, into a prelude for – of all things – a satirical playlet based on the 75-minute *Macbeth* that the playwright Pavel Kohout and the actor Pavel Landovsky were presenting in Prague through their illegal 'Living-Room Theatre'. *Dogg's Hamlet, Cahoot's Macbeth*, which Berman quite properly regarded as 'one play, one evening', presents our creative playfulness as the harmonious ground of both language and liberty.

Stoppard made several changes in *Dogg's Our Pet* to turn it into the first part of *Dogg's Hamlet*. No longer does the script simply posit a workman who discovers that he cannot understand his own partner's language. That 'Charlie' now becomes one of the schoolboys, whose chatter begins to lead *us* into their language of Dogg. Soon, however, 'Abel' and 'Baker' begin to rehearse without much comprehension a dialogue in Shakespearean English from the opening of *Hamlet*. Only then does a modern Englishman arrive – a lorry-driver for Buxton's Deliveries, in white boiler suit and cloth cap, who brings the planks, blocks, slabs and cubes for constructing the wall and platform. (Or does this 'Easy' in Stoppardland or on the other side of the Linguistic Looking-glass just *dream* that he has met a tribe of short-trousered lunatics whose words often mean the reverse of what they seem to say? He tries to tell them that his mate 'got struck down in a thunderstorm on the A412 near Rickmansworth – a bizarre accident . . . a bolt from the blue, zig-zagged right onto the perforated snout of his Mickey Mouse gas mask'. Did that bolt stun Easy, too?) Though baffled at first by the language of Dogg, Easy soon experiences a linguistic breakthrough. He becomes able, as we are, to grasp a few insults and commands, count up to twelve, and announce the school's performance of 'Hamlet bedsocks Denmark'.

In the school ceremony, which still includes the Lady's apparently scatological encomium, all of the trophies have been won by a teacher's pet, Fox Major, who will now play Hamlet. Dogg, the schoolmaster, himself plays Claudius; an added Mrs Dogg plays Gertrude; Charlie plays Ophelia, using in the mad scene a bouquet of flowers mislaid at the ceremony; and puppets now replace the imaginary players in the dumb-show. The set consists of the newly built wall and platform, folding screens, and some ludicrous cut-out props. Though the text of the 15-minute *Hamlet* remains substantially the same, its meaning changes with this new context and cast, and it now contributes to the larger whole that is *Dogg's Hamlet*. With Easy, we had entered a linguistically bewildering but tacitly familiar dramatic world. As we began to learn its language, we found the inhabitants themselves trying to learn a Shakespearean language already (in some sense) at our command. Their absurd condensation of *Hamlet* now suggests a woefully inadequate grasp of its tragic richness; but it is also, of course, a lightly satirical comment on our own reductive schooling. Nevertheless, we have experienced here the fact that human beings can transcend all such differences between worlds through a playful education in language.

Because that possibility is crucial to the next playlet, the entire evening is also more than the sum of its parts. *Cahoot's Macbeth* begins with thunder and lightning, and the three witches chanting in near darkness. But the first scene of *Macbeth* glides smoothly into the third as Macbeth and Banquo arrive; and when the witches vanish and the lights come up, the action continues in what is now obviously a living-room with shuttered windows. This undeniably serious condensation of Shakespeare's script proceeds without interruption as far as Act II, scene 2. When Macbeth enters with blood-stained daggers, we hear a police siren approaching – and then hear the knocking that we now doubly expect. 'Wake Duncan with thy knocking!' says Macbeth. 'I would thou couldst.' The next character who enters, however, is not the Porter but an Inspector who asks with sarcastic politeness: 'Oh – I'm sorry – is this the National Theatre?' *Cahoot's Macbeth* (like Shakespeare's) has suddenly become both more ominous and more absurd. As a Hostess now comes forward through the audience to intercept the Inspector, the tragic style seems to become enclosed within a Pirandellian realism. But this Inspector, who intends to smoke out something very like Kohout's forbidden 'Living-Room Theatre' in Prague, is a more sinister version of Stoppard's earlier Inspectors Hound, Foot, and Bones. His heavy wit declares him a character out of some black comedy who has arrived to squelch the high tragedy with which we are in cahoots. Amid these collisions of style and tone, some surprising correlations between *Macbeth* and its enclosing action begin to turn Shakespeare into a subversive playwright.

The Inspector's allusion to a 'rough night' serves as an unintended cue for Macduff, who enters with his lament: 'O horror, horror, horror! / Confusion now hath made his masterpiece!' The Inspector soon requires the play to continue, and the actors reluctantly proceed – their playing-style, in BARC's rendition, approximating a rather heavy 'walk-through' of the script. At the end of Act II, however, with the announcement that Macbeth has 'gone to Scone/To be invested', the Inspector chooses to applaud 'a happy ending'. That clinches the analogy between Macbeth's usurpation and the 'normalisation' of Czechoslovakia. When the Inspector says that 'intellectuals' are now 'in the doghouse', Banquo, who is played by Cahoot, at once goes into an imitation of a dog. (Behind the verbal humour here is a rather complex allusion. Cahoot's howling and barking repeat the lucidly lunatic behaviour of Kohout's own *Hamlet* actor, Kerzhentsev, in *Poor Murderer* (1972), who says: 'Why should a human being without conventional scruples – that is, a normal human being – if he suffers like a dog, not howl like a dog?') Asked for a statement, Cahoot speaks Banquo's lines at the beginning of Act III: 'Thou hast it now: King, Cawdor, Glamis, all/As the weird sisters promised . . . .' The Inspector orders all to leave (with a 'Nice Dog!' for the still growling 'non-person' Cahoot) and exits. Then Act III begins in earnest – so to speak.

As soon as two murderers prepare to ambush Banquo, complications of another Doggish sort begin. The shutters open and Easy appears at the window, announcing himself in Dogg as bringing a load of blocks. The surprised murderers smoothly incorporate him into Shakespeare's script: Easy becomes, for the duration of the scene, the third murderer. He is then led off by the Hostess, but he returns during the banquet of Act III, scene 4, hovering at the fringes of the action in Macbeth's eyeline whenever Macbeth 'sees' Banquo. For us – and, we must assume, for the Czech actors – Easy in his white boiler suit has become an unexpected ghost. When he returns again after Act IV, scene 1, the lights come up and the cast interrogates him. He tells again of his bizarre accident on the A412, but now in Dogg ('Blankets up middling if season stuck, after plug-holes kettle-drummed lightly A412 mildly Rickmansworth . . .'). Indeed, he seems now unable to speak 'English'. But we glimpse a ratio here: English is to Dogg in *Dogg's Hamlet* as Dogg is to 'Czech' (which we hear as English) in *Cahoot's Macbeth*. Easy has a phrase book this time, however, and has increased his skill in imitative learning. When he repeats the assertion, 'We speak the language', he is in fact beginning to speak the language.

Act IV, scene 3, begins with Malcolm and Macduff lamenting the fate of Scotland. But with 'Bleed, bleed, poor country!' we hear again the police siren. And soon, instead of Ross, the Inspector arrives once more. ('My countryman; but yet I know him not,' says Malcolm.) Responding to Macduff's question about the state of Scotland, the Inspector has his own fun with languages: 'Cahoots mon! Where's McLandovsky got himself?' But at this point Easy introduces himself in Dogg, provoking a linguistic confusion that subsides only when Cahoot enters – for that self-styled dog does himself understand Dogg. 'Where did you learn it?' asks the Inspector. 'You don't learn it, you catch it,' says Cahoot. (And indeed, the Hostess has already been catching it: 'He's got a two-ton artichoke out there.') When the Inspector again orders everyone to clear out, the cast responds by beginning Act V in high theatrical style – and in Dogg. 'Hat, daisy puck!' exclaims the sleep-walking Lady Macbeth, 'Hat, so fie!' An off-stage policeman listening to this bugged room calls the Inspector on the phone to find out what is happening. 'How the hell do I know?' expostulates the Inspector. 'But if it's not free expression, I don't know what it is!' Easy, however, can now recognise *Macbeth*.

As Act V proceeds in Dogg, Easy and members of the

cast unload the blocks (the woods of Birnam are indeed moving) and begin to build the platform and steps as in *Dogg's Hamlet.* We recognise Macbeth's most famous speech – 'Dominoes, et dominoes, et dominoes, / Popsies historical axle-grease' – and Macduff's challenge: 'Spiral, tricycle, spiral!' But the play's climax now contains several confrontations and reversals. The Inspector interrupts Macduff's advance, mounts the now completed platform, and delivers a scatological tirade. Using a kind of linguistic judo, however, Cahoot understands the Inspector's 'English' as Dogg and applauds his friendly tribute. The Inspector then calls in two Policemen, who begin to build a jail-like wall of grey slabs across the proscenium opening. But Macduff again challenges Macbeth (and by implication all usurpers) and proceeds to kill him. The phone rings again, and this time Easy (Birdboot-like) answers it, as Malcolm mounts the platform and places Macbeth's crown on his own head. Malcolm's final speech in Dogg dovetails with Easy's response on the phone, which is sliding from Dogg back into our own English English. Over the fanfare he shouts: 'Double double toil and trouble. No. Shakespeare'. And after a pause: 'Well, it's been a funny sort of week. But I should be back by Tuesday'.

Replaying the situation of Rosencrantz and Guildenstern in their utterly mysterious Elsinore, Easy's adventures in the worlds of Dogg, Shakespeare, and Prague now make explicit the triumphant meaning of our playful presence even in scripts that have decreed our absence. Indeed, as Jack Kroll said, Stoppard has here performed 'the extraordinary feat of affirming art, life, and freedom in trumpet-tongued gibberish'. That gibberish is clearly the antithesis of the artificial bureaucratic language, Ptydepe, which dominates the characters in Havel's satirical play *The Memorandum.* But it is also, in effect, a surprising mutation within the genre of English melodrama. A popular entertainment in nineteenth-century England was the 'dog-drama', for which plays of all kinds were adapted to include canine protagonists. There was even a 'dog-*Hamlet*', in which Hamlet's dog, always at his side, listens to the ghost, observes the king, watches the duel with Laertes, and at Hamlet's dying command leaps at Claudius' throat and kills him. For Stoppard – by way of the language-games of Lewis Carroll and Ludwig Wittgenstein, the theatre-games of Ed Berman (Professor R. L. Dogg) and the histrionic ingenuity of Kohout himself – that dog has become Dogg, a natural, playful, and contagious language of co-operation that enables us to surmount if not destroy the grey walls of usurping tyranny.

Having completed four plays that address 'topics of the day', Stoppard told Robert Berkvist in 1979 that he had 'no sense whatsoever that a fifth play would be a natural successor'. He was 'just not sitting here thinking, "From now on, I'm such and such kind of writer" '. Indeed, if there is a natural succession in Stoppard's plays at mid-career, we must find it in the contrapuntal variety that has always energised his distinctive but omnivorous style. That fact emerges clearly from the strikingly different adaptations he has most recently prepared for Peter Wood and the National Theatre.

Stoppard had adapted Mrozek's *Tango* in 1966 and Garcia Lorca's *The House of Bernarda Alba* in 1973, had completed screenplays of Thomas Wiseman's *The Romantic Englishwoman* in 1975, Nabokov's *Despair* in 1978, and Graham Greene's *The Human Factor* in 1979, and had adapted a fourth novel, Jerome K. Jerome's

Three Men in a Boat, for television in 1975. His work of this kind attained its highest level of distinction, however, in his adaptation of Arthur Schnitzler's play of 1911, *Das Weite Land*. That ironic anatomy of Viennese decadence allows the highly civilised games of love and honor to expose their own hypocrisy and their deathly emptiness. For Schnitzler's often quietly oblique dialogue Stoppard found a deft English equivalent, re-creating what he called 'the mysterious collusion of sound and sense which gives a writer his distinctive voice'. He did not deny himself, however, 'a flick here and there' to charge the conscious and unconscious role-playing of Schnitzler's characters with a further increment of dry wit; and he chose for the play a title that recalls the soliloquising Hamlet's evocation of death. *Undiscovered Country* opened at the Olivier Theatre in June 1979, with John Wood as Friedrich Hofreiter and Dorothy Tutin as Genia. Reviewers found that Stoppard had brought into the English repertory a most impressive play – and one that, in its subtlety of psychological and social portraiture, provides a major (if collaborative) extension of his own stylistic range.

Stoppard added more than an occasional 'flick' to his next adaptation, a free-wheeling treatment of a very different kind of play. Johann Nestroy's farce of 1842, *Einen Jux will er sich machen (He'll Have Himself a Good Time)* is itself an expansion of John Oxenford's one-act play of 1835, *A Day Well Spent*. Nestroy's pompous grocer travels to Vienna to plight his troth to a charming but easily impressed woman, and to prevent his niece and ward from marrying her suitor. He leaves his store in the hands of an assistant and an apprentice, who take the opportunity to go out on the town themselves. During their adventures they encounter their master but elude discovery, and the plot builds until almost every character on stage is posing as someone else or believed to be someone else by some dupe. In 1938 Thornton Wilder chose the play as a vehicle through which to spoof the conventions of melodramatic staging. Setting aside Nestroy's rich Viennese dialect, he moved the action to New York in the 1880s, added the character of Dolly Levi, who manages to win the grocer for herself, and produced *The Merchant of Yonkers*, which he slightly revised in 1954 as *The Matchmaker*. That play, with further revision by Michael Stewart and songs by Jerry Herman, became in 1964 the extraordinarily successful musical *Hello, Dolly!* Undaunted by this history of adaptation, Stoppard decided (on the urging of Peter Wood) to provide yet another version of what he called Nestroy's 'almost mythic tale of two country mice escaping to the town for a day of illicit freedom, adventure, mishap and narrow escapes from discovery'. Updating the plot by some fifty years, he thoroughly Stoppardised its farcical language and action. He gave characters distinctive verbal tics, loaded the script with a razzle-dazzle of puns, malapropisms, double entendres, mistranslations, and other linguistic high-jinks, and incidentally turned Vienna into a city that, having lost its head over not Cahoot's but Verdi's *Macbeth*, is 'overrun with Scottish capes, kilts, tam-o'-shanters . . . and highland flingery of every stripe'.

On the Razzle opened in September 1981, at the Lyttelton Theatre. Michael Billington applauded its 'relentless comic zest'; Peter Hepple praised 'a newly-created comedy of sheer delight'; and Robert Cushman declared: 'From political farce and philosophical farce Mr Stoppard has turned to writing farcical farce: both a raging example of the genre and a tribute to it'. But there were also reservations, as there had been when Wilder seemed to be wasting a distinguished talent on someone else's quite unintellectual material. Kenneth Hurren found this

Stoppard 'an embarrassingly long way from the writer who dazzled us in *Jumpers* and *Travesties*'. Sheridan Morley, acknowledging a 'triumph of energy and eccentric invention', saw no good reason 'why our most distinguished comic dramatist should have been spending his recent time cobbling some new jokes into a dog-eared plot'. And Benedict Nightingale asked: 'How could he squander so many clever, non-reusable lines on what is – let's say it – an enterprise at best frivolous, at worst confused and silly?'

The linguistic lunacy of *On the Razzle* does invite such praise and such doubts. In more than two decades of writing, however, Stoppard has shown that playful variety can provide both immediate energy and long-term direction, and that for a master of incremental repetition nothing need be wasted. Stoppard's characters, styles, and plays may spin off like eccentric catherine wheels, but they soon disclose themselves to be luminous points in a relatively coherent galaxy. Nor would he be averse in principle to letting a more 'substantial' play reuse lines from *On the Razzle*, just as *Jumpers, Travesties*, and *Dogg's Hamlet, Cahoot's Macbeth* had built upon earlier plays by himself as well as others.

Some critics have been dismayed by this predilection for pastiche and parody. Andrew Kennedy, for example, has emphasised the 'precariousness' that results from Stoppard's lack of any 'approximate norm of theatre style': 'For the question is whether full parodic theatricality, in its licensed interplay of pastiche as dialogue, can possibly find room for anything so grave as a centre of gravity'. The answer to that question should now be fairly clear. Stoppard's contrapuntal procedures find ample room for what is far more surprising and illuminating than your ordinary centre of gravity: centres of levity that contain their own implicit aesthetic and ethical norms. Regardless of subject or style, every Stoppard play celebrates what Sophie in *Artist Descending a Staircase* calls 'a world that includes itself'. It invites us to affirm the artist's playful ability, our corresponding ability to share in his exploration of an often bewildering world in which people can do terrible things to each other, and the freedom and moral sensitivity that are necessary conditions for this collaborative play. We should not be surprised if Stoppard now shows himself able to veer away from the farcical overloading of *On the Razzle* to something quite different – a 'straight' play, perhaps, about a 'serious' situation in Poland. In any event, as he continues with his zig-zag exploration of the values and commitments implicit in his levity, he will surely find gravity enough.

Notes

1. Centres of Levity

The early reviews by Ronald Bryden and Harold Hobson are quoted by Kenneth Tynan in *Show People* (New York: Simon and Schuster, 1979), pp. 73–4. Stoppard's remarks to Mel Gussow appear in 'Stoppard Refutes Himself, Endlessly,' *New York Times* (April 26, 1972), p. 54, and 'Stoppard's Intellectual Cartwheels Now with Music,' *New York Times* (July 29, 1979), Section D, p. 22.

2. Anxious Stylists

The quoted reviews of *Enter a Free Man* are: Mary Holland, 'Cards of Identity,' *Plays and Players* (June, 1968), 23; J. W. Lambert, 'Plays in Performance,' *Drama: The Quarterly Theatre Review*, No. 89 (Summer, 1968), 25. Stoppard's remark to Janet Watts appears in 'Tom Stoppard,' *The Guardian* (May 21, 1973), p. 12.

3. Playing Our Absence

Martin Esslin's remark about *Rosencrantz and Guildenstern Meet King Lear* is quoted by Ruby Cohn in *Modern Shakespeare Offshoots*

(Princeton: Princeton University Press, 1976), p. 211. The quoted reviews of *Rosencrantz and Guildenstern Are Dead* are: John Chapman in the New York *Daily News* (October 17, 1967), reprinted in *New York Theatre Critics' Reviews*, 1967, p. 255; Martin Gottfried in *Women's Wear Daily* (October 17, 1967), reprinted in *New York Theatre Critics' Reviews,* 1967, p. 256; John Russell Taylor, 'The Road to Dusty Death,' *Plays and Players* (June, 1967), 13, 15; Walter Kerr, 'The Comedy that Kills,' *Thirty Plays Hath November* (New York: Simon and Schuster, 1969), pp. 51–3.

4. Logics of the Absurd

Robert Benchley's remark is reported by Kenneth Tynan, *Show People,* p. 87. Ed Berman's and Tom Stoppard's comments on *Dogg's Our Pet* appear in Berman, ed., *Ten of the Best British Short Plays* (London: Inter-Action Imprint, 1979), pp. xi, 80. Berman's account of the misplacement of *The (15 Minute) Dogg's Troupe Hamlet* is in the same volume, p. x.

5. Ethics and the Moon

The quoted reviews of *Jumpers* are: Martin Gottfried in *Women's Wear Daily* (April 24, 1974), reprinted in *New York Theatre Critics' Reviews*, 1974, p. 300; Howard Clurman in *Nation* (May 18, 1974), p. 637; Clive Barnes in *New York Times* (April 23, 1974), reprinted in *New York Theatre Critics' Reviews*, 1974, p. 299; Jack Kroll in *Newsweek* (May 4, 1974), reprinted in *New York Theatre Critics' Reviews*, 1974, p. 303.

6. The Prism of Travesty

W. H. Auden's comments on *The Importance of Being Earnest* are contained in 'An Improbable Life,' *New Yorker,* 39 (March 9, 1963), 155–77, reprinted in Richard Ellmann, ed., *Oscar Wilde: A Collection of Critical Essays* (Englewood, N.J.: Prentice-Hall, 1969), pp. 111–115. Peter Wood's remarks about *Travesties* appeared in the *London Times* (June 8, 1974), and are quoted by Ronald Hayman, *Tom Stoppard* 3rd edn.; London: Heinemann, 1979), p. 117. The quoted reviews of *Travesties* are: Clive Barnes in the *New York Times* (October 31, 1975), reprinted in *New York Theatre Critics' Reviews,* 1975, p. 170; Howard Kissel in

Women's Wear Daily (November 3, 1975), reprinted in *New York Theatre Critics' Reviews*, 1975, p. 168; Jack Kroll in *Newsweek* (November 10, 1975), reprinted in *New York Theatre Critics' Reviews*, 1975, p. 171.

7. Language, Lunacy and Light

Stoppard's remark to Janet Watts appears in 'Tom Stoppard,' *The Guardian* (May 21, 1973), p. 12. The reviews of *Dirty Linen* are: Martin Gottfried in *New York Post* (January 12, 1977) and Walter Kerr in *New York Times* (January 23, 1977), as quoted by Felicia Londré, *Tom Stoppard* (New York: Frederick Unger, 1981) p. 127. Stoppard's remark to Robert Semple appeared in *New York Times* (June 21, 1976), also quoted by Londré, *Tom Stoppard*, p. 128. Stoppard's note to *Every Good Boy Deserves Favour* appears in the Faber and Faber edition of that play and also on the jacket of the RCA recording. Mel Gussow's review of *Every Good Boy Deserves Favour* appeared in *New York Times* (August 1, 1979), reprinted in *New York Theatre Critics' Reviews*, 1979, p. 195. The quoted reviews of *Night and Day* are: Harold Hobson, 'Hobson's Choice,' *Drama* (N.S.) No 131 (Winter, 1979), 44–5; Douglas Watt in the New York *Daily News* (November 28, 1979), reprinted in *New York Theatre Critics' Reviews*, 1979, p. 83; Howard Kissel in *Women's Wear Daily* (November 28, 1979), reprinted in *New York Theatre Critics' Reviews*, 1979, p. 85; Walter Kerr in *New York Times* (November 28, 1979), reprinted in *New York Theatre Critics' Reviews*, 1979, p. 82; Jack Kroll in *Newsweek* (December 10, 1979), reprinted in *New York Theatre Critics' Reviews*, 1979, p. 87. Stoppard's remarks to Robert Berkvist appeared in 'This Time, Stoppard Plays It (Almost) Straight,' *New York Times* (November 25, 1979), Section D, p. 5. The quoted reviews of *Dogg's Hamlet, Cahoot's Macbeth* are: Mel Gussow in *New York Times* (October 4, 1979), reprinted in *New York Theatre Critics' Reviews*, 1979, p. 146; Douglas Watt in the New York *Daily News* (October 4, 1979), reprinted in *New York Theatre Critics' Reviews*, 1979, p. 144; Clive Barnes in *New York Post* (October 4, 1979), reprinted in *New York Theatre Critics' Reviews*, 1979, p. 145; Christopher Sharp in *Women's Wear Daily* (October 5, 1979), reprinted in *New York Theatre Critics' Reviews*, 1979, p. 145; Jack Kroll in *Newsweek* (September 24, 1979), reprinted in *New York Theatre Critics' Reviews*, 1979, p. 148. Ed Berman's remark to Robert Berkvist appeared in 'In Cahoots with Tom Stoppard,' *New York Times* (September 30, 1979), Section D, pp. 3, 9. The quoted reviews of *On the Razzle* are: Michael Billington in *The Guardian*, reprinted in *London Theatre Record*, I (1981), 492; Peter Hepple in *The Stage and Television Today* (October 1, 1981), p. 13;

Tom Stoppard

Robert Cushman in *The Observer,* reprinted in *London Theatre Record,* I (1981), 490; Kenneth Hurren in *What's On In London,* reprinted in *London Theatre Record,* I (1981), 494; Sheridan Morley in *Punch,* reprinted in *London Theatre Record,* I (1981), 491; Benedict Nightingale in *New Statesman,* reprinted in *London Theatre Record,* I (1981), 494.

Select Bibliography

(i) Works by Stoppard

'Reunion', 'Life, Time: Fragments', and 'Story', in *Introductions 2: Stories by New Writers* (London: Faber and Faber, 1964).

Lord Malquist and Mr Moon (London: Faber and Faber, 1980; New York: Grove Press, 1975).

Rosencrantz and Guildenstern Are Dead (London: Faber and Faber, 1968; New York: Grove Press, 1967).

Enter A Free Man (London: Faber and Faber, 1969; New York: Grove Press, 1972).

The Real Inspector Hound (London: Faber and Faber, 1968).

Albert's Bridge and *If You're Glad I'll Be Frank* (London: Faber and Faber, 1969).

A Separate Peace (London: French, 1977).

After Magritte (London: Faber and Faber, 1971).

The Real Inspector Hound and *After Magritte* (New York: Grove Press, 1975).

Jumpers (London: Faber and Faber, 1972; New York: Grove Press, 1972).

Artist Descending a Staircase and *Where Are They Now?* (London: Faber and Faber, 1973).

Albert's Bridge and Other Plays (New York: Grove Press, 1977).

Travesties (London: Faber and Faber, 1975; New York: Grove Press, 1975).

Dogg's Our Pet and *The (15 Minute) Dogg's Troupe Hamlet*, in *Ten of the Best British Short Plays*, ed. Ed Berman (London: Inter-Action Imprint, 1979).

Dirty Linen and *New-Found-Land* (London: Faber and Faber, 1976; New York: Grove Press, 1976).

Every Good Boy Deserves Favour and *Professional Foul* (London: Faber and Faber, 1978; New York: Grove Press, 1978).

Night and Day (London: Faber and Faber, 1978; New York: Grove Press, 1979).

Dogg's Hamlet, Cahoot's Macbeth (London: Faber and Faber, 1980).

(ii) Recording

Stoppard, Tom, and André Previn, *Every Good Boy Deserves Favour* (with Royal Shakespeare Company and London Symphony Orchestra), RCA Records (ABL 1–2855 Stereo, Red Seal) 1978.

(iii) Adaptations by Stoppard

Schnitzler, Arthur, *Undiscovered Country* (London: Faber and Faber, 1980).

Nestroy, Johann, *On the Razzle* (London: Faber and Faber, 1981).

(iv) Articles and Interviews by Stoppard

'Something to Declare', *The Sunday Times* (February 25 1968) p. 47.

'Ambushes for the Audience: Towards a High Comedy of Ideas', *Theatre Quarterly*, IV, No. 14 (May–June 1974) 3–17.

'But for the Middle Classes', review of *Enemies of Society* by Paul Johnson, *Times Literary Supplement* (3 June 1977) p. 677.

'Prague: The Story of the Chartists', *New York Review of Books*, XXIV (4 August 1977) 11–15.

Gordon, Giles, 'Tom Stoppard', in Joseph F. McCrindle, ed., *Behind the Scenes: Theater and Film Interviews from the 'Transatlantic Review'* (New York: Holt, Rinehart and Winston, 1971), pp. 76–87.

Hardin, Nancy Shields, 'An Interview with Tom Stoppard', *Contemporary Literature*, XXII (1981) 153–166.

(v) Checklists

Ryan, Randolph, 'Theatre Checklist No. 2: Tom Stoppard', *Theatrefacts* 2 (May–July 1974) 2–9.

Carpenter, Charles A., 'Bond, Shaffer, Stoppard, Storey: An International Checklist of Commentary', *Modern Drama*, XXIV (1981) 546–556.

(vi) Criticism: Books

Bigsby, C. W. E., *Tom Stoppard* (London: Longman Group for British Council, 1976).

Cahn, Victor L., *Beyond Absurdity: The Plays of Tom Stoppard* (Rutherford, N. J.: Fairleigh Dickinson University Press, 1979).

Dean, Joan Fitzpatrick, *Tom Stoppard: Comedy as a Moral Matrix* (Columbia, Mo.: University of Missouri Press, 1981).

Hayman, Ronald, *Tom Stoppard* (3rd edn. London: Heinemann, 1979).

Londré, Felicia Hardison, *Tom Stoppard* (New York: Frederick Ungar, 1981).

(vii) Criticism: Articles and Portions of Books

Ayer, A. J., 'Love Among the Logical Positivists,' *The Sunday Times* (9 April 1972) 16.

Cohn, Ruby, *Modern Shakespeare Offshoots* (Princeton: Princeton University Press; 1976, pp. 211–217.

Cooke, John William, 'The Optical Allusion: Perception and Form in Stoppard's *Travesties*', *Modern Drama*, XXIV (1981) 525–39.

Crossley, Brian M., 'An Investigation of Stoppard's "Hound" and "Foot" ', *Modern Drama*, XX (1977) 77–86.

Crump, G. B., 'The Universe as Murder Mystery: Tom Stoppard's *Jumpers*', *Contemporary Literature*, XX (1979) 354–68.

Davidson, Mary R., 'Historical Homonyms: A New Way of Naming in Tom Stoppard's *Jumpers*', *Modern Drama*, XXII (1979) 305–13.

Ellmann, Richard, 'The Zealots of Zurich', *Times Literary Supplement* (12 July 1974) p. 744.

Gabbard, Lucina P., 'Stoppard's *Jumpers*: A Mystery Play', *Modern Drama*, XX (1977) 87–95.

Gold, Margaret, 'Who are the Dadas of *Travesties*?' *Modern Drama*, XXI (1978) 59–66.

James, Clive, 'Count Zero Splits the Infinitive: Tom Stoppard's Plays', *Encounter*, XLV (November 1975) 68–76.

Kennedy, Andrew, 'Natural, Mannered, and Parodic Dialogue', in *Yearbook in English Studies*, IX (1979) 28–54.

Keyssar-Franke, Helene, 'The Strategy of *Rosencrantz and Guildenstern Are Dead*', *Educational Theatre Journal*, XXVII (1975) 85–97.

Marowitz, Charles, *Confessions of a Counterfeit Critic: A London Theatre Notebook, 1958–1971* (London: Eyre and Methuen, 1973) pp. 123–126.

Tom Stoppard

Tynan, Kenneth, *Show People* (New York: Simon and Schuster, 1979) pp. 44–123.

Zeifman, Hersh, 'Tomfoolery: Stoppard's Theatrical Puns', in *Yearbook of English Studies*, IX (1979) 204–20.

Index

Index

Index

Index

176

Index